LITTLE RIVER OF AMAZEMENTS

New and Selected Poems

by

Mary Kay Rummel

BLUE LIGHT PRESS ◆ 1ST WORLD PUBLISHING

SAN FRANCISCO ◆ FAIRFIELD ◆ DELHI

Little River of Amazements

Copyright ©2024 by Mary Kay Rummel

All rights reserved. Printed in the United States of America. No part of this book may be used or reproduced in any manner whatsoever without written permission except in the case of brief quotations embodied in critical articles and reviews. For information contact:

1st World Library
PO Box 2211
Fairfield, IA 52556
www.1stworldpublishing.com

Blue Light Press
www.bluelightpress.com
bluelightpress@aol.com

Book & Cover Design
Melanie Gendron
melaniegendron999@gmail.com

Interior Illustrations
Melanie Gendron

Cover Art
Conrad (Tim) Rummel

Author Photo
Lisa Baird

First Edition

Library of Congress Cataloging-in-Publication Data

ISBN: 978-1-4218-3557-0

PRAISE FOR MARY KAY RUMMEL'S POETRY

"Her book is a shimmering display of light and a search for what matters."

– Diane Frank, novelist, poet and editor of Blue Light Press, author of *While Listening to the Enigma Variations*

"One suspects this collection might best be looked on as a long search for prayer – a search anchored in the certainty of the loving heart. These are mindful, watchful poems where beauty seeps into the world with the subtlety of a Monet painting."

– James Silas Rogers, poet, essayist, author of *The Collector of Shadows*

"Mary Kay Rummel's poems have and sustain an oracular voice."

–Stanley Kunitz, Poet Laureate of the United States, author of *Passing Through*

"Mary Kay Rummel's writing is mature, lyrical, and intense."

– Linda Gregg, poet, author of *All of It Singing*

"The passionate journey of a woman in search of illumination."

– David Mason, poet, author of *Incarnation & Metamorphosis: Can Literature Change Us?*

"Mary Kay Rummel, much like some 8th century Irish scribe, perched on a high bench near a window, has not only observed the ever-changing light of the world, she has pressed her ear to the pthalo blue lips of Heaven and made her own luminous manuscript, fantastical and full of music."

– Jackson Wheeler, poet, author of *Swimming Past Iceland*

"About the poems in MK Rummel's book – she writes about travel, love/sex, family (the dead and the living), god and goddess, but what I love is the way the poet approaches these subjects: the poignancy of a young heart hidden under a veil and the bird's joy in escaping the cage."

– Sharon Chmielarz, Poet, author of *Duet in the Little Blue Church*

"Thanks to the beauty and resilience and strength of the natural beings all around us and inside us too, in need of us speaking on their behalf. That's what she does in her poetry, reconnecting us with Being and meaning."

> – Maia, Poet, author of *Portraits* and *See You in Our Dreams* (Speculative Fiction)

"Her gift to the reader is an exhilarating sense of having traveled far without leaving the heart's house."

> – Thomas R. Smith, poet, author of *The Glory* and *Medicine Year*

"Mary Kay Rummel takes us on a pilgrimage – as much of mind as of language – past the natural world's apparent surfaces and into those places that flash with a spiritual resonance that, the poet assures us, we have only to believe in and they will be discovered. Rummel's is no easy faith, however: body is ever restive, soul elusive, light is equally illumination and darkness that gets traded for yet more darkness. Which is to say, the poems correctly temper hope with honesty, conviction with clarity of vision."

> – Carl Phillips, poet, essayist, author of *Scattered Snows, to the North: Poems (2024)* and *My Trade Is Mystery: Seven Meditations from a Life in Writing*

"In body, mind, heart and spirit, Mary Rummel's poetry evokes the fire of transcendence. Her poems, so beautifully and eloquently layered, give readers the thrill of surprise as they find themselves in her words. Like a cat's cradle of green laser beams – green is the color of transcendence – Mary Rummel shines the light on what's eternal and unknown."

> – Jean Colonomos, poet, playwright, author of *Living the Dream*

"Reading Mary Kay Rummel's poems is more important than ever. I read her poems to remember how spiritually connected we are to each other, no matter where we are on this planet. Her poems express her spiritual journey. Color, light, music, and art, are woven into these poems that read like psalms. In one poem, she writes, "Lapis lazuli, original blue mined from earth/in Afghanistan, ground to aquamarine of illuminations,/found in the teeth of a medieval female/ scribe, ground to paint the Virgin's gown in centuries of Annunciations." In another poem, we journey with her to Paris, the Notre Dame Cathedral, and again to St. Paul, Minnesota where she is from, to end the poem: "A surge of strings against the night. /Past present future one smooth stone." We can›t ignore what is happening in the world. Rummel reminds us to focus on finding beauty, and transform the chaos into hymnal music."

    – Clauda Reder, poet, author of *How to Disappear*

"Mary Kay combines a palpable sense of the world "out there" with a strongly registered fullness of personal consciousness. In her work, a sacramental notion of the world merges in continuously interesting ways with a more directly secular apprehension of self. What I noticed and like about so many of her poems is the way they give tangible expression to a state of being that seems close to what we mean when we use the word "faith". The experience of faith lies, I guess, at the edge of speech, of language. In her poems, however, she gives subtle and satisfying expression to it."

    – Eamon Grennan, poet, author of *Selected and New Poems*

INTRODUCTION

An introduction to this collection of poems selected from books written over almost thirty years is really a gratitude list for more people than I can name here. I am amazed that I was able to create this work and it could not have happened without the encouragement of others. Special thanks to Pat Barone for sharing her editing skills.

Thanks to my parents who modeled and encouraged reading. Sister Mary Honor, in junior year English at St. Joseph's Academy in St. Paul played a BBC recording of *Murder in the Cathedral* by T.S Eliot. I was blown away by the drama, the sound of the language, the power of poetry to inspire. After that, I began to try to write poetry. During typing class I made up poems instead of doing the assigned pages. It was the beginning of a long life of doing poetry when I was supposed to be doing something else. I began to understand how to think as a poet, how to catch the connections, how to create and name my life through language.

Thank you to the teachers from the University of St. Catherine and the University of Minnesota who encouraged me. In these developing years poetry became a way of weaving together all the disparate threads of my life as wife, mother, teacher, writer, and seeker of the spirit. Onionskin, the Twin Cities writing group that still meets, helped me keep writing during the years when I was pulled in many directions. These poets taught me faithfulness to the task. Thank you to pianist Gwen Perun for the many lovely music-poetry programs that we have performed.

In 1985-86 I received a Mentor Award from The Loft Literary Center which changed my life as a poet. Linda Gregg showed me how to think of myself as a public writer. Bill Truesdale of New Rivers Press encouraged me to keep applying for the Minnesota Voices Award until I won it with my first book. John Judson of Juniper Press and Betty Rossi of Loonfeather Press also were mentors, publishing many of my poems in the journals they edited and then publishing my books.

I have deep gratitude to the administrators, colleagues and friends from the University of Minnesota, Duluth for their support during the time I was on the faculty there.

After I came to California to teach at CSU Channel Islands, I connected with Diane Frank, founder of Blue Light Press. Her online workshop was just what I needed at the time. Working with Diane and becoming part of the Blue Light Press community of poets has once again changed my life as a poet. This book is a result of that collaboration. Special thanks to Melanie Gendron, book designer for Blue Light Press, whose elegant drawings have enriched this book and earlier books.

The other great part of my new life in Ventura, CA was meeting great poets of the southern and central coast especially Phil Taggart and Marsha de la O, Jackson Wheeler and David Oliveira. Ventura was the center of a lively community of poets and they welcomed me. I was so honored when I was asked to be the first poet laureate of Ventura County. This experience made me especially conscious of the communal aspect of being a poet. I am still working with poetry in community through the Ventura County Poetry Project, a non-profit for the support of poetry. In California, I also became part of two writing groups, Summer Women and the Salonistas, which keep me going as a writer. Thank you to them.

Thank you to the friends and relatives who have come to my readings and supported my books through the years. And I want especially to thank my husband, Conrad (Tim) who has been there for me through it all; my sons Timothy and Andrew their wives, Miranda and Ann; my four granddaughters who are my inspirations. I can't thank all of you enough for your support over these years and for helping me see more deeply into the meaning of love. I am still faithful to the task.

Mary Kay Rummel

*I understand greed for life, why most of us die
still wanting more
— a little more.*

– David Oliveira

LITTLE RIVER OF AMAZEMENTS

Contents

New Poems

Part 1. For the Speechless World

Adamantine	1
Ocean's Edge	2
Seven Ways to Change the Names of the Days	4
Pelicans in the Rain	8
Hope in All Things	10
Winter Solstice in Big Sur	12
River, Stone and Stars	14
Diagrammer of Sentences	16
Life is Losing and Reinvention	18
Bat	20
Sonata for Gulls and God	21
Son et Lumiére: Chartre	22
December Bodies	24
Witches' Solstice	26
Hugging Bridget After the Pandemic	27
Winter Hearts: A History	28
Sometimes the World	30
Writing the Names of the Days	31
Wheatfield With Crows, Vincent Van Gogh, 1890	32
Old Ceremonies	34

Part II. Against the Dark

Bridges	37
Done	38
Remember the Port of Cassis	39
My Cartographic History	40
A Brief History of Love	41
Lightning at Solstice	42
Against the Dark: A Poem Sequence	43

There's No Hour	44
Visitor	45
Eighty	46
Welcoming Night	47
If Trees: A Call and Response	48
Sycamore in Autumn	50
With the Memory of Water	51

From *This Body She's Entered*

Above Them Both	55
Seamstress	56
Letter to a Former Mother Superior	57
Our Inheritance	58
How She Leaves	60
Cambridge, England, 1986	62
In the North	63
Of Circles and My Sons	64
Step on a Crack	66
Talking With a Window	69

Poems from *Green Journey, Red Bird*

Birches	73
How to do the Ropes Course	74
A Little Helper	76
Red Bird in Winter	77
River Cop	78
Heron	80
Symbiosis	82
Boatyard, Late October	83
Night Birds	84

Poems from *The Illuminations*

Histories	87

In the Margins of the Pages	88
Cairns	95
Family Stories in London	96
Translations	98
The Name of Destination	99
In the Middle	100
A History of Rain	103
La Azotea: a Rising Wind	104
In All Our Fasts	106
The World a Folding Book	108

Poems from *What's Left is the Singing*

As If	111
This is my Body	112
Memento	114
Van Cliburn in the Convent	116
The Oak	118
Parakeet	120
Patterns of Obedience	122
Coming Home	124
Surfacing	126
Blue Webs	128
Beginning With Skin	131
Catch and Release	132
Names for Green	133
What's Left is the Singing	134

Poems from *The Lifeline Trembles*

Wounded Angel	137
Ars Poetica	138
Lost: A Sister's Tale	140
Gardens of Paris	142
A Beltane Tapestry	144

The Unicorn Tapestry: *a mon seul désir* 145
What Stone Knows 146
Palimpsest 147
California Morning Song 148
Both Ways 149
The Poet Goes Fishing 150
Between Rivers 151
Field Walking in County Donegal 152
Istanbul Winged 153
Aging in Ephesus 154

Poems from *Cypher Garden*

The Open Window 157
Cypher Garden 158
Haiku Ladder 160
Season of the Swan 162
Remembering Paris: A Poem Sequence 164
   White Nights 164
   Meditation in Notre Dame Cathedral 165
   Carrying a Green Branch 167
   Sunflower 169
Thundering Up West Seventh 170
By Way of Words 172
Praise 174
The Gift 175
Mother Tongue 176

Poems from Nocturnes: *Between Flesh and Stone*

After Basho 179
Illuminator Dreams 180
Nocturnes 182
Finding Her: Mother Goddess on her Throne 5750 B.C. .. 184
Still Life with Lemons, Oranges and a Rose 186

Roses and Monks: Birmingham, England 187
The Songs 188
Finding Blue 190
Vanishing 192
Derry in Time of Brexit 194
There is a bell inside this memory 196
Starlight on Waves 198
Stone and Desire 199
In a Time of Distancing 200
Blue Distance 201
Our Story 202
A Medieval Herbal 204
Blueing 206
From Water 208

Publication Acknowlegements 211
About the Author 215

New Poems

I

For the Speechless World

Adamantine

Holding a stone in my hand –
a hard river stone worn smooth by water,
what a river does to granite over time.
Holding solitude in my hand.
Holding silence like a rock.

On my wall a Chinese painting –
clouds drifting over peaks,
a waterfall tumbling down a cliff.
To the side, a little bridge over a creek.
A rounded figure crossing over,
about to disappear into mists.

In a long ago autumn dusk
the crows called my name.
I rose from my life, left everything –
past, home, parents.
I almost turned back to my mother,
had another destination beyond the frosted fields
filling with night.
Seeing the deer, ghostly in moonlight,
my first vision of solitude,
I moved into silence.

The sky thins.
The world tightens like a walnut.
Air snaps off like a twig.
I can count what I love
like stones in my hand.

Ocean's Edge

Swimming up from sleep,
I hear wind shake the window frame,
watch for the welcome streak of rain
across the glass and when it's over,
walk to the gray Pacific.

Kelp tangles, dark on the beach,
stripe the sand. My feet explode
tiny bulbs of sea wrack. Just offshore,
a seal shows me how to ride a wave,
to surface on granite, spread
on rock to dry.

My grandmother, that strong Kerry woman,
rocked in her chair and told me of seals,
selkies who take the form of women,
then change into seals again.

Some are your cousins, children of Maura,
captured on the rocks off Dingle.
They married, had children,
then returned to the sea.

Today a selkie points to the beach.
Here yellow marigolds and glowing
gorse bushes light the walk
among patches of purple heliotrope.
Look for light patterns, she says,
how it's dark beneath them.

A shaft of light slants through the mist,
sends arrows into the waves,
singles out a patch of vineyard

on the mountainside.
Look every day.
Where life began, it begins again
in the waters that hold you.

Then she dives, leaving me on shore
remembering how my grandmother
ended her story:
Someday you will go there, and you will know
the truth of my words
more lasting than the wealth of the world.

Seven Ways to Change the Names of the Days
 After David Horovitz – *Changing the Names of the Days*

1. Paint a minute

Maybe if I stand at the end of the pier
each day at sunset while clouds and sky
explode into orange and fuchsia,
colors I think belong to Guatemala,
try to match my breathing
to the filling and emptying of waves,
I would not be so afraid of living
or of loss.

I could let the day go the same way
I welcome it each morning –
wave-loved, undercut by time,
washed away in light.

The rocks are faces eaten away
by cavernous weathering.
All night the sea pounds.
Roaring rivers travel ley lines of earth.
Water, rock, dreams – all metamorphoses –
the beauty of what is absent.

2. Write the familiar

Royal blue iris wave in sea wind –
my eyes swim in their purples,
holy icons like the Van Gogh irises
on a red wall.
These sacred faces with soft yellow centers,
goddesses of the human courtyard.

3. Read a book written by a tree

How can I name the light
that so clearly shines from bark in spring?
When a sycamore grows its leaves,

I see the candles underneath,
the twisted elegance of laced branches,
the roughness, the cuts, the smell
of a thing breathing inside itself.

4. Be a tree librarian

Ghost dance of sycamores
against light shot sky,
live oak leaves tremble and shine.
Owls fly into the sleeping woods
where the osprey opens its wings
and the book closes.

The librarian believes the sound of a saw
is a slit of the tree's tongue,
but its throat song echoes.

5. Go In Deep

Dismantle what
      the heart knows
Redefine this mourning
      so it will be morning.

Break through lost days
      into today
Marriage into marriage
      into marriage.

Wade into it deeper
        mouth deep.

Unlearn perfection
Unlearn romance
Unlearn the sentence
        to hear each word
the constellations
        to see the stars.

A new landscape
        old tracks washed away
The river unwinding.

Travel the wildness
        in that sweet body
to get to the body inside
        the body you thought you knew.

6. See through the eyes of a crow

Was I ever a girl the way she is, studying at the table,
her eyes sliding away from her notebook?
Those untamed eyes lead her to the crow,
its dark, far-seeing eyes.

Her hands obey, then disobey, the open book before her.
Without knowing why she longs to write outside
ruled-lines, off into the margins of space and time,
outside English, opaque mother-tongue,
throwing shade the way clouds darken windy days,
concealing foxes, brush rabbits, twin fawns, wild iris.

Wordless things. Deep live things.
The girl-with-crow's eyes
finds them, wants to draw them.

7. Look now, go on looking

without any turning away –
into all the speechless worlds
poised to leave us.

Pelicans in the Rain

*A single lifetime is not long enough
to know even a single moment* – Claude Monet

Wild mustard mends the mountains.
Gulls climb the wind.
I watch the sun's shape turn
from sphere to palace,
burning but not disastrous.
I want to honor the invisible,
use the rising fog to see young
egrets pecking between rocks.

Sea-tide turns sand to rippling mirror,
the way Monet changed the pond
at Giverny back into the dream it really was –
hay-stack clouds, willow-cathedrals,
incandescent melting candles of lilies.

Just before sunset, sundogs flare
across the sky then quickly fade
behind clouds.

The landscape blurs into invisible gifts –
what we see when we stare long enough
into emptiness.
A pair of white pelicans glide
out of rolling mist and are gone.

Like the old masters, I seek
a shape for rain,
the way Monet and Debussy captured rain,
trying to measure a quiet too pure
and transparent for humans.

Not splatter, parallel hard
but rain itself, the way it sends gladness
from sky to my fingers.
A quick memory wings,
and the instant takes its dazzled form.

Hope in All Things

    After *Spem in Alium, (Hope in all Things)* – Thomas Tallis

I remember how the heavy doors
opened into a great silence.
At the base of each arch in the gothic chapel
a singer waited until one voice, bell-like,
began the melody.
An alto joined, then another voice, until forty voices
gathered in the clarity of the round,
until the song crested
in a wave rising to the vaulted ceiling.

I learned how hope inhabits sound,
the way cricket-throb scree-slides over miles of air.
My ears ring a moment in answer to the fox
prowling the ridge of Anacapa Island.

I listen for hope in what surrounds:
the four sounds of the ocean –
beneath the train, the drum, the rain-stick
sift of water, a high trill.
The quiet shape of rain in drought
opens a salt-rusted door.

A deep center opens
like the passage between rocks on Anacapa –
music on the knife edge of the world,
where hope grows.

Here, every listener surrenders
to the sound and rhythm,
each voice brushing against,
ringing the bells of, another.

In free air it is possible to hear
a more than human language
crescendo – tide gold
as the island boat rides out,
on the eternal round of sea.

Winter Solstice in Big Sur

Between every tree and its story
is an opening to night.
I want to bend down
to taste the sacred minerals.
I send up prayers
and they float away.

Between every dance
of air is a departure.
Raising my arms
I face the moon and bow,
breathing with trees
in the circle of redwoods.
Their silence a murmuration –
a wave of evergreen and pine
surrounds my fear,
fills my emptiness.

Between every circle and its rim
is a call lapping at the roots.
I hear this call the way I sense the cold path
when clouds obscure the moon,
then clear above the circled crowns
of thousand-year-old redwoods.

Through the high branches
a passage for solstice light,
ring of planets,
corona of black, gold and rose
making the old moon young.

Between mountains and rivers of wind
a tree shivers at the edge.

Night shadows I cannot know,
but there is time, still, to search
for translucence, the pearl-sheen of life.

Between insomnia and sleep
trees singing in cold air.
Songs only the old and very young can hear.

River, Stone and Stars
Rocky Mountain National Park

1
Cassiopeia, you are above the mountain –
as if the mountain is your floor,
the night sky the walls of your room.
We look up as if by looking we could climb,
as if we were light.

2
If I stay a long time by the rushing river
when Cassiopeia is low and her lines
repeat the black geometry of the mountains,
it's not just she that holds me,
but the worship I learned as a child
in dark churches that shut her out.
Can I live for a week in a state of prayer
or is it passion that makes me pledge to walk
the distances ahead, trusting rock cairns
for direction, stacked by other hands.

3 *for Tim*
Constellations of mica
on canyon walls.
Stars, granite firmaments
thrust upward until they fall.
River and boulder merge here
like the place we meet –
deep inside each other,
where once again we defy falling.
Old love liberated, feathered, flying.

4
Water-shaped stone
wave-shaped stone
I polish with my fingers
stone of endless steps.

Stone of vigilance.
Stone I brought home, fossil filled.
You are the stone from dreams
where a nun shadow asks,
Which stone will you choose?
Which life?

Diagrammer of Sentences

Carry a sentence across the night – David Horovitz

In the corner of the living room,
huddled over my pink wooden desk,
brothers fighting, mother angry
because I'm not peeling potatoes,
I'm wandering in English homework.

Find the stately subject, a proper start.
What am I – subject or object?
Find the predicate,
its leaping, chaotic verb.

Seven of us crammed close
in that small house, bracing against
winter winds, luminous ice tricks.

Modify, shape, change.
Could words change my family?
There is language here –
Celtic roots, English derivations,
West Seventh slang.

My mother first gave me words,
but now when I write my own spells
she reads my journal,
destroys my grave, erotic notes.

Wind bangs against the house
in conditional tense.
Cold sets in our pavid bones.
My mother, argus-eyed –
worries scribble her face,
loneliness, a cave in both of us.

*I want, I pray, I think –
how to parse a labyrinth of longing?*

I take my pen and diagram
a live tree, a sideways tree,
a sentence all my own:
*I lived another time,
in a deep world beyond myself.
I will live there again.*

Life is Losing and Reinvention

Often a nun comes in a dream.
I walk into a Spanish church.
She stands at the altar
and waits for me, arms outstretched.

And have you found God yet?

    Once I knew where to find God.
    Just sit in the wooden pew,
    feel the paths in the wood
    beneath my hands and watch
    the little house on the altar,
    the red light signaling he was in,
    a god small enough to fit in there,
    large enough to save the world
    and me in it.

Where did you stop along the way?

    On the feast of St. Joseph
    we walked into the chapel in bridal white
    and the bishop gave us new names.
    Our sisters led us out.
    Later we returned in black
    all but faces covered.
    I believed everything I did
    had meaning.

Then why did you walk away?

    It was a cold love we had,
    the unacknowledged
    parts of us fresh and safe.

We worshipped an old god-man
like the one in renaissance paintings,
loving that red wine smell,
his eyebrow hairs sticking out
like the legs of spiders.

Have you stopped searching then?

Later, in love, I thought a man in me
Was god – his being taking up my whole,
the hands that held me, God's hands.

I thought to find God when our bodies
fed upon each other but didn't I know better?

I think more likely the sea is God,
deeper than this past I dive into
looking beneath these bodies.

Now I ask you –
why are we told there are no Gods,
and why do we still look knowing
they will surface if we feed them?

We are more alike than you want,
my mother, your mother,
you and me.
Women can't be possessed.

Life is losing and reinvention.
Isn't it? Isn't it?"

Bat

Curled up in a corner of the chapel ceiling
like a god's shuttered eye,
it waited as I was waiting
for the call of a hundred singing women.
Join us, join us in the same milk breath.
I held a candle and vowed my fierce young life.

The mitred bishop on the altar steps,
priests in a row behind him.

Veni creator spiritus, we all chanted
wanting to be blessed
when, swooping across the sanctuary,
the bat circled the tall hat of the bishop.

This leather-winged, wild heart
was night shade, frantic,
midwifed by darkness.
My pulse hummed and I knew
where to find my own body's shadow
among all the women in black.

Veni, we sang, and it came to us,
like the crazed spirit of a light-stunned god.

Sonata for Gulls and God

I will pray this morning
like a clear violin.
My hands' scherzo
the conductor.
My body's adagio
of arcs, angles, angels.

I will hear this morning
the sonance of light,
gulls with grit tipped wings.
Stand on my bare toes,
watch many mountains
move across the sea.

Always searching for
the beloved face,
I'll play the waves
a bass full of flood.
Gulls swerve, their cries cold
in light-laced air,
in sun-struck turns
loosening feathers so others
grow in their place.

I lost the old God I was given
at birth – who rewarded
and punished;
who was there each morning
and now is gone.

Son et Lumiére: Chartre

Walking the medieval city,
buildings crumbling and black,
rows of blowsy yellow roses, I feel
cracked old walls absorbing heat.

Outside the great Cathedral,
I lean back far enough to glimpse
workers scraping scaly soot
from stained glass.

Inside I study pantheons
of light and blue illusion
where the Madonna seems
to look on me with kindness.

In her window she floats in lapis lazuli
of a southern sky, while sunlight falls,
burning, like this moment, from inside out.

When my mother at eighty was dying,
she asked me to be sure my father
didn't marry that woman from church
who wanted the money she'd let him save
instead of giving her the new kitchen
she longed for.

I'm sorry now that I laughed
knowing it would never happen.
My mother fought against the hardest thing –
letting go, letting go
as the seas rose in her lungs.

Now I hold mother, father together
in my body and in my mind – a talisman.
Here, across a rising sea from home,
I feel closer to them. And to her.
Beside these walls I feel like a child
holding shards of history,
blessed by the sacred haloing of light
as it falls through the Madonna,
through her sea's twelfth century cobalt.

Tonight's offering, light and music
near the great Last Judgment doors.
Angel acrobats will fly across stone faces
of the saved and lost.

I'll wake in the morning,
cold, neck-sore, stiff-boned –
these things tell me the world is *here*
saying goodbye.

December Bodies

White pelicans in the estuary
bless the shallow Ventura river
with their stillness
before it disappears
into sun swept Pacific.

Then it's gone –
the little river of amazements
curved through sand, swallowed by sea.
Waves roll over, a last thin swerve
where fresh water meets salt.

A ribbon of gulls skim those waves
like foam, white in the morning sun,
brushed with pink at sunset.
On what's left of sand
one hunched figure – driftwood
or the lifeless body of a seal
holding on to this bit of earth.

Thirty white pelicans, shore watchers,
dropped like snow, reminding me
of Christmas in my below-zero childhood
near the radiator, my mother dressing
under her nightgown in front of the grate.
Seeing her heavy breasts, I feared
for my own bird-slender body.

White pelicans float in place,
rest on a sandbar,
frenetic gulls all around them.

Their soft whiteness suggests
falling petals of the winter rose
called moonstone –
snow on the distant mountains
visited by the moon.

Witches' Solstice

What do they say about us –
women who dance, who chant?
What do they say about
the ceremonies of our bodies,
our innocence of flesh?

Scrying, we see the cities in ruin
toads with pulsing throats on the walkways.
Walled gardens surrounded by sand
lions guarding the gate.

We dance in the music of the present.
above the setting canoe moon
wreathed in sunset pink.

Worshipping Jupiter and Saturn – lovers
moving slowly toward each other
for eight hundred years,
the power of their conjunction.

In the dark wood we praise the meadow,
sunlight on blue hills,
the valley that used to be home
where the bear eats night's fallen apples,
then rolls down the road to sleep.

Near the holy well a grey sign says
If your prayer is for the dead
Walk over the stream,
If for the living
Walk through the water.

The apples are dry, the she-bear sleeps.
The stream bed awaits our feet,
sings our new and ancient ways.

Hugging Bridget after the Pandemic

All year her quick hands
made small altars of stones.
Branches blossom
wherever she streaks
across the grass stirring treasures
from matted leaves.

I am a house full of crickets.
She folds into my hollows,
candled and warm,
crawling back
into the original story.
The curled frond where life began
begins again.

Winter Hearts: A History

Praise the fire-building storytellers

My brother Bill, a legendary trekker,
loves to sleep in snow caves like a bear.
Once in Yellowstone he and Tim skied
backward down the trail when they disturbed
a grizzly sleeping in her cave.

Praise old fears that shift and stir

Like the black bear I met
on that path in Duluth,
a shadow until she slid
into the moon limned yard,
sending the dogs
into paroxysms of barking.
She ate the last apples,
fighting against sleep.

Praise weather, extravagant and wild

During the great Halloween blizzard,
a sea of snow rolled over Duluth.
Alone in an old house, I wore a path to the window,
watched a few figures struggle to the liquor store,
a snowmobile, a plow in the dark.

Marooned, I remembered the summer bear
that rolled in from the woods each night
to sit in the sandbox next door.

Praise that ice-caked highway

In the morning, between winds, a grey sludge,
a hole where there had been rocks and beach,
I heard and felt but could not see Superior,
wanted to drive south even though nothing
with wheels was moving.

Praise snow lovers

I never wanted to be on the Bear Tooth Pass in a white-out.
I was searching for moose and found
a family of them leaping in twelve feet of snow –

bull moose, new antlers starting to grow from velvet,
dreamed of a head like a tree running into wind.
Grandfather moose with a long beard
danced toward the road where I clung to my snowmobile,
five year old Andy attached to my waist.

I think of snow-mobilers trapped on this pass
who burnt check books, dollar bills to survive.

Praise winter hearts

Like mirrored lakes
where clouds and water freeze together,
up and out of the dark
the cold pulls a garden of crystals.

Sometimes the World

In the sand I saw a strange blend of softness
and brittle energy in a shattered wing,
and the blue that floated beneath the surface
of its feathers – sometimes flesh is a window.

As I moved away gulls came down,
out of the sky – a blizzard,
to stand fussing in a circle
around their dead companion.

The tide came in,
lifted that broken body upon its hem,
an untidy white mass appearing,
then vanishing, with each swell.

Dolphins circled,
disturbing fish in their deep schools
while wings of pelicans flashed,
their dives parting bright air.
A fishing boat turned around
and headed toward open sea.

The gulls waited on shore facing west.
Mostly silent. Keeping vigil.
One of the times this world
is close enough to paradise.

Writing the Names of the Days

When I'm walking each day beside the Pacific,
I'm exploring caves in Cappadocia,
where early Christians painted their story on dry walls,
desert sky splotched with bright dots of hot air balloons,
riders looking down.

I'm walking in blinding California sun,
but in my mind I'm reading Yeats to my cousins
beneath the glowering mountain, Benbulben.
As we circle the poet's grave, my 86-year-old aunt cries.

Today, I'm warm on the beach, but my body remembers
the walk in Minneapolis across the Stone Arch Bridge
over a frigid Mississippi where spray from the dam crystalizes.
Above me faces of playwrights flash on black
walls of the Guthrie Theatre.

Between the ocean and its chaotic crash,
between what I lived then and now,
a coruscation of light from a dark center –
a singing   a stutter   a spell
each memory breathing inside its own fragrance.

As I walk in rhythms of arrival and departure,
the osprey writes circles on the sky,
its whistle a message from another world.

Today death is a suitcase
stored away.

Wheatfield With Crows, Vincent Van Gogh, 1890

What can one do...but gaze upon the wheat fields...
for we who live on bread, are we not ourselves wheat...
– Vincent Van Gogh 1889

Vincent paints all day in the wheatfields,
dipping into bruise blue, molten gold,
piling on in ecstasy, painting
his heart's solitude and terror.

Nearing death, he paints unrelenting crows
clawing the sky over wheat.
Sky spiraling with crows' dark warnings.

Our lives, momentary
as if I am waiting, ticking time
and if I am grieving tears, thick and sure
as fading sheaves of wheat,
is it too soon?

Too soon, calls a crow
Too late, calls another.

We send the heart out,
day after day,
willingly and in terror.
Vincent writes, *I am ravished,*
ravished with what I see.

He paints that spatter of crows
furling out over wheat,
drags them wing by wing into his sky;
our own bodies trapped without wings.

Our stubborn bodies a harvest –
the only home for the heart –
even as hot wind
billows the dust we are,
and carries it away.

My heart has nowhere else to go.
A crow is perched inside my eye
as if it means to stay.
Is it too late to tell me now?

Old Ceremonies

Now that the grass shivers with insects,
now that the air is a hive of light,
now that dragonflies are mad with sex
in hanging gardens of wisteria

Isn't it time to name the colors of our life
the way Mayans wove hibiscus,
papaya and jade into cloth?

How can we turn away?
The trees are inscribing fifty names for green.

Let's walk west along the slant lit shore,
watch the sea blossom into lavender,
an illuminated book of hours.

Let's paint each other
in the book of breathing,
in the ceremony of opening
of the mouth, of the body,
the ceremony of leafing.

We are alive, still in love,
       running out of time.

II

Against the Dark

Bridges

Nheng, our friend in Bangkok, had been up all last night, carving colored soaps into petaled flower gifts for us. Tonight, on the river boat, she orders the rainy season foods she loves. We swallow luminous lychees, eat fish baked whole, scoop it from the bones. The Chao Phyra River reflects spires of golden wats and skyscrapers, tiny houses almost tumbling into the water. Night hides dark apartments with kitchens hanging off the back. From the shore drift smells of jasmine, frangipani and garbage while we pass long boats, dark ferries, rice barges and couples who ply the river selling fresh crabs and fish to boaters. Around us, singing Thais. When we pass under bridges the young men cheer the way our children did when we drove under bridges, and before that, the way my brothers and I yelled from the back seat of my father's black Chevrolet, *honk the horn*, our hands raised to hold up every wooden railroad trestle in St. Paul. The shouts a memory bridge, from there to here.

> In Bangkok I saw
> a man ride an elephant against traffic
> on the expressway.
> Beneath a wooden railroad bridge,
> all of us hanging on from here to there.

Done
After Maureen McClane

My glass of *vinho verde* sparkles in Portuguese sun and, sadly, it is almost done, this meal near Sagres, once called *World's End* by sailors of all religious belief. I stick a fork into *Sultan's Delight*, lamb stew served with a silky aubergine puree. Its many origins brine my tongue. I'm thinking about the merchant republics, knowing they are done. And so is the nun who forbade us, aged six, to say we were done. She mimed opening the door to the oven where we were thoroughly roasted. *If you are done that means I can stick a fork in you,* she said. *You,* she corrected, *are finished.*

Sister Archangela terrified us, first graders who were thrust into the world of nuns pledged to Christ and torture of wayward souls. In second grade, we stared in horror when Sister Mary Patrick, her twin, walked into our class, *There's another one!* We were done for. Wimpled nuns, dressed in wool, were they multiplying?

> I was a nun but those days
> are done and I'm almost done
> almost historical as a ship
> heading west to steal gold for kings.
> I stick in my fork and I eat, I eat.

Remember the Port of Cassis

Remember the port of Cassis
where we sailed along the sea carved cliffs
and after the beach crowds left
had dinner at a small table,
the restaurant on the top of a hill street,
cobblestones beneath our feet,
whitefish with *beurre blanc,*
Rhone Valley wine.

The waiter was Andre, his mother the cook.
Old love came alive in that place,
color at the heart of everything.
You left our table to take a photo,
Mediterranean in gentian light,
one sailboat slicing cobalt water.

That night in our small room
your body, my palette,
my body, your canvas –
we called all the colors,
the sea's thousands of little fires.
Amethyst, turquoise, sapphire
burned inside us.

My Cartographic History

I never learned to read a map.
I had no need of one on West Seventh
or on my restricted convent walks.
You were young and impatient
and I just wanted to lie
near any campion spun from stone.

Did it matter after all?
How we missed the Jungfrau,
how we made love on the wrong mountain.

We found another vertical meadow,
lay on alpine forget-me-nots,
near an abandoned shepherd's hut.
We were surrounded by a parade of peaks
one of them the Jungfrau we never knew.

Old maps were never enough;
it's time to let them go.
These days I try to name each rock, bloom, bird
while you long for any mountain.
In this weathering of spirit, our lives,
snowbound and crowned with stone,
we are mapping our own Jungfrau,
a cartography of the heart

A Brief History of Love

In each other's arms on that mountaintop,
we thought we might live forever
in portraits and self-portraits called memory,
in a cavern always being painted,
large enough for our souls to sleep in.

We make one promise after another
to the surprise love makes of sacrifice.
Everything gone returns.
The cold rose cajoled back into bloom.
The white pillar of winter sunlight
we can, at last, look at together
without fear of burning.

Love is spacious here –
moonlit ghost ship, oil platform,
indigo horizon –
where I stand beneath the stars,
then go inside to your arms,
again and again, returning.

The way the heart pounds and pounds
for as long as it does, the way it seems
we will always be like this –
the season of flowering beginning again,
a hum at the back of the throat.

Lightning at Solstice

A crack in the sky
splinters the willow,
fresh gold slash against green.
Into the hollowed trunk I pour
my prayers.

*Don't let his body be bitten
by the red backed spider.
Don't let lightning singe
the roots of my hair.*

Every June night, toad basses
punctuate the peeper chorus.
Firefly rhythms break the dark.

Mornings, green heron
fishes from the fallen trunk,
hunching reddish neck and head
over brackish water.
Baby mallards float
light ribbons behind their mother.

Summer air agrees with
lilting arias of orioles
singing to each other as they loop
from oak to cottonwood.
Already, they trill, *already*
while the grey phoebe chants
her base note –
not yet, not yet.

Against the Dark: A Poem Sequence

When will the lights go on
in the house
I carry wherever I go?
One light for the kitchen
where the soup-pot steams,
one for my sons
bent over their homework,
one for the dog as he licks his dish,
one for my husband as he builds a fire,
one for my father who comes no more,
one for my mother, my brother, my nephew,
and one for me.

Will each light,
lead us home?

There's No Hour
   for my father

Is it because I still think I am immortal?
There's no hour
of the day or night I'm afraid of.

I love morning's surprise of gold light,
the blue silk rustle of evening,
and the night air as I study the lights of the city
while damp seeps down from the hills.

Some hours, my father keeps me company.
His caring comes to visit me from deep inside myself.
I can feel his love as if he were standing,
in his usual silence, hands in his pockets, watching me.
His smile rests on the summer air,
remains in slow night darkness.

Sometimes, I think about the hours
of his last morning,
hours so immense with solitude.
I keep leaning into them
as against a tree
being uprooted over and over.

Visitor
for my mother

A first bird flies across the morning.
I sit waiting for the mist
to unravel above the river,
for the blue asters to shake off dew.

All of these things have happened before,
so why should she not also
come back up the walk toward the house,
hyacinths in her hand.

Or if not my mother, then the deer
that slipped out from the oak trees
after she died – and walked in her steps?

Eighty

Thousands of pelicans fly west.
Long braids unravel across cerulean sky
or they skim – almost surf – waves,
brushing foam, ponderous wings
sometimes disappear below the curl.

Ungainly pelican grace enters
my arthritic bones – clumsy outsider
in this grace-filled world
of sea and sun-washed limbs.

Years weigh me down.
Streams of light carry me
through charging surf, draw my mind
into the green-lit cove at the center
of each diminishing swell.

Welcoming Night

I'm learning to let the dark
into my house, my body, my soul,
to let trees show me night is a scouring
strong enough to smooth rock.

I'm learning to let the night in,
the way it engulfs those cottonwoods
on the hill across the pond.

Sometimes darkness comes inside hungry,
pulling a leash that's tied to an oak.
I try to welcome its growl and roar.

On midsummer evenings as dark crawls
up trunks to crowns,
there's a letting go, a slow reversal.

Tops of old trees hold
the yellow moon while around me
roots quiver – silence, their talk.

Tonight I watch fireflies weave
across a black scrim of leaves –
the blink of my time in air.

If Trees: A Call and Response

If the willow trembles
before the wine-rich drink of earth,
> *we can taste holy and joy,*
> *shallows sweeping*
> *at the shore of our feet.*

If oak trees not yet fully awake, still dream
of spring in a cloud of mist,
> *they take notice of us*
> *same as any dragonflies*
> *or leaf-brushing robins.*

The maple leaves flutter
in one handed applause,
but if those branches reach toward each other,
if leaves from birch and cottonwood
brush even on windless days,
> *so can we, in that quiet.*

If they create a nave where we can pray,
energy sparking between them,
yellow shining with rain,
cardinal sparking the understory,
> *we can enter there*
> *in our isolation*
> *listening to leaves stroke*
> *each other inside wind.*

If this night is a woodland,
> *trees seize the earth intimately.*
> *Seeds sow themselves*
> *spinning into rose gardens and lava fields.*

If this night orchard grows,
>   *we can grow with it, rooted*
>   *in deep waters, reaching for light.*

If we hang our coats with their overflowing pockets
from low branches in the grove
where the oaks stand in a circle,
>   *their world so much larger*
>   *becomes where we live.*

Sycamore in Autumn

In an aura of terror and delight,
spirit haunted, caught.
The more you gaze at it, the more
it trembles. Each fold dissolves
into an ever thinner veil
less and less of what you see –
not in, but through the tree.
The river behind it shimmers
more insistently in the sudden flicks
of light between the disintegrating
leaves and asks, *what's left?*
What matches this fierce shivering and shedding?
How will you clamber through
to vibrating silence which shakes,
shakes from your old skin,
your worn-out, greying self-that-was,
and sets you loose,
naked and glowing?

With The Memory of Water

Washing my face with the memory of water...
– Tongo Eisen-Martin

You are walking beneath an arch of cottonwoods,
thinking, *This could be anywhere
in the world, any nation's capitol,
and I could be anyone.*

The red kiosk, the five-dollar flowers,
a man kneeling on the sidewalk,
hands clasped in prayer:
It will all be right.
You understand the traffic,
the woman throwing soda cans,
the crane preying
over a new building.
You say *excuse me, thank you*
and feel you're speaking in tongues.

Then you remember how the waves beat
the sand like blood in your veins;
how you read the gulls' compulsive hustle
like a page in a familiar book.
You saw tracks on the beach,
dark striations of a tide-bed map,
hundreds of small ponds reflecting the sky.
You remember how you said to yourself, *yes,*
and did not know the word for *why.*

From
This Body She's Entered

*...and you knew that you stood on the brink of that sea
that was neither charted nor plumbed by men,
that sea-shore only women had known, dark with its sailing
red lights of storms, where only the feet of women had trod,
hearing the thunder of the sea in their ears as they gathered
the fruit on that waste, wild shore...*

A Scots Quair by Lewis Gibbon

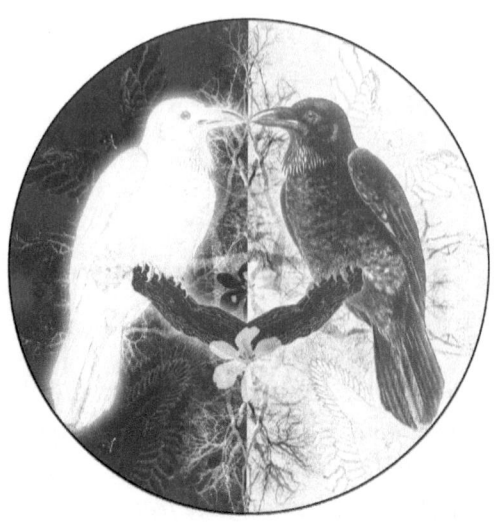

Above Them Both

I am painting my wall.
Let the mother have a corner,
the one who sits outside
preparing corn and beans.
Her children run in and out
of her mouth, protected,
sent out, protected again.

Let the nun have a corner,
the last in the long line
of black robed women
who brought me to this time.
Because I absorbed their prayers,
I grew their chants for feet.
Because their hungers carved
the caves of my stone face,
I grew curved with a cup for a belly.

Above them
I paint the loon.
All arrowhead and feathers,
silvered moons on black wings,
shot from the water's bow.

Today, I straighten to fly
on new found winds.

Seamstress

I remember a sewing machine,
a black Singer with a pedal
that tapped all afternoon
beneath my grandmother's foot.
Her thick fingers pushed cotton
and silk into its snapping mouth
until her eyes darkened from strain.
Parades of bright dresses,
shirts, shawls tumbled from her machine.
On our thin bodies,
we wore her eyes.

In the mirror
I see my mother's face
and my grandmother's face,
a long parade of Irish Marys
with tunnels for eyes,
holes where children crawl,
eyes made blind
from too much looking
at the sea.

Afternoons
I feed my typewriter
raw fear and strange words –
the cotton pieces of my life.
They step out whole
and walk away on thin legs,
solid like mirrors
with eyes wide open.

Letter to a Former Mother Superior

In a drawer in the kitchen
onions kneel
circling their cut cords.
In the parable
a man puts time in a bank
then grows so aware of seconds passing
the earth begins to spin beneath him.
He lies on a couch and counts time –
insects thick in the air.

Dear mother and sisters
I must confess –
last week I broke silence
fifteen hundred times.
And I still break it,
smash it like a coffee cup.
The brown eye of silence
stares from the floor.

I walk to a stage
to give a poetry reading,
look up to find the eyes of my friends.
The audience is all nuns,
pale faces folded in stiff wings.
They come to claim me
these tellers of silence.

Our Inheritance

All over Europe on last-judgment portals
of medieval cathedrals, lust with his grinning belly
and ass head, carries women to damnation,
nude women slung over his shoulder,
their hair hanging long.

On the left side of the main portal
of Chartres Cathedral, place of the lost, the damned,
one woman walks, is not carried, not nude, a nun,
all but her face veiled.

She smiles as she walks,
a message to generations of neck sore women.
As if she is saying, "It was worth it,
like nothing that ever happened before."
      I love to look at you, he said,
      to talk while I am loving you.

I closed my body for a long cold season.
In one brief transit I opened for him.
      You smell so good to me, he said.
      I love to taste you.

He loved my body.
With him my body was my soul.
      I love to listen to your small sounds.

I wanted to swallow him
in me, one heliacal rising.
On my knees in cold mornings,
I tried to exorcise him.
In the night when I beat my flesh
his face grew on my thighs.

In this city of God built by men
whom can I ask for forgiveness?
Why would I, who have broken out
of this book of glass written by men,
come back to the same death?

These circles that open into God
close down on a woman who knows
that body and soul are one.

How She Leaves

1
When she looks into water she sees
her own face whole – then breaking again.

When she looks into water
she finds her own shattered eyes
mending.

She forced those eyes to stay open
when they longed to close.

You may see her bright and calm,
but it's the dark lake
cold and wild that she loves.

2
In a boat on Whitefish Lake
she and the loons watch the day ending.
Beneath her the blue grey belly
of yesterday's rain.

She watches as if her life did not
depend on watching, as the sun
bleeds spasms of color,
until the blue veil carries light away.

Loons wear darkness, night covers their heads –
they shake the stars with their grief.
Their cries in the night are hers.

3
In the northern summer night
silence is borne in the bodies of trees

that hover between two tributaries
as if they could choose which to enter.

Hills, trees, undersides of leaves
sway in lean and clouded light
where she floats into sunlight, into shadow –
snags a rock, hesitates, whirls away again.

It isn't the leaving that counts.
It's the freedom to do it.

4
Just when she thought she could
jump into clear water, get her hair wet,
say straight out what she wants –
she's snagged by fear and begins to struggle.

She's wounded by God's silence –
arrow in the chest, just missing the heart.

5
She carries it inside her.
Loons play wounded on the water.
Raising high pitched alarms, they become
floating black islands in the vast lake.

> *Come take us, they seem to say*
> *can't you see we're weak.*

Then her eyes follow as they lift
as if shot from the water's bow –
black northbound arrows.

Cambridge, England, 1986
For Tim

An old mill pub
hangs low over the River Cam.

From its walls willow
streamers trail brown water.

I think of you
how you love this slow beauty

the way the cloud
loves its slice of moon.

It swells you the way
history fattens up this lazy river

lives in you
a language that walks your walls.

Today my willow hands
remember the press of you

the earth gone rural
thatched with words that bind us.

I come to hear Romeo woo Juliet
where once we walked green-eyed.

I know I would not die for you
but I'd consider it.

In the North

I buy my son
a small canoe paddle

at night
he comes into my room

it is the paddle
not the water he needs

I wonder
where is he going

that the paddle
held wide like a wing
can take him?

Of Circles and My Sons

> *I saw how the planets gathered*
> *like the leaves themselves*
> *turning in the wind.* – Wallace Stevens

This poem is for Timmy
for he is onion mouthed.
His words can make me cry.
He describes and catalogues each moment,
a geologist examining the ancient hills.
His words like round bodies of birds
hit my windows in October and fly
away without being dazed.
For he winters without me
and returns in spring,
growing shadows
only slightly familiar.

This poem is for Andy
for he is radish warm,
a flamingo in his cool home.
He runs like a mouse scurrying
his voice a tail dragging behind him.
He swims outward turning his head backward.
He sees earth and flowers
in the frosted winter windows.
His hand fits in mine as a place
where it plans to stay.
He never travels far.

I don't know yet if we are leaves
swirling in a great wind
or the wind itself.
We dance around each other
in ever growing orbits.

We wear each other
like tight rings
impossible to remove.

Step on a Crack
I don't want to be like you: I want to be holy. – Jan MaGrane

Young girl:

I don't want –
>step on a crack
>and you'll break
>your mother's back
>a voice warns in her mind

I don't want to make you angry
but I don't want to be
>a mother of boys
>a cleaner
>a cook.

I don't want to be like
>the white haired women
>in house dresses.

I don't want a double chin.
I don't want to lose a breast.
I don't want to be like you –
>serving my dad and brothers.

I don't want to be like you
>who cares about me.

I want to be like
>Joan, Virgin and Soldier
>Teresa, Virgin and Scholar
>Maria, Virgin and Martyr

those women who really knew how to suffer.

Her mother: (years later)

Daughter,
We have fought our way to this –
>the beds you wouldn't make
>the jobs you wouldn't take
>the men you wouldn't date

because you didn't want to be like me.
And here you are with me again
in the place you left.
You telling me that now you know
I was always holy and strong,
honest about my scars.
I'm afraid of you now.
I won't let you touch them.

Daughter: (somewhat older)

Mother,
I dream you walk away from me
to a womb-like place where crowds
have gone before you.
Such grieving, raging crowds,
like the TV faces at foreign funerals.
I think you will be trampled by them.
You grow tinier.
I can't see my mother in you;
I see my child.
As you get close to the place
you walk taller and disappear
with the straightening.

You couldn't teach me how to be
the woman I chose,
but you show me how to be old –
how to choose life when dying
looks easier,
that something in us grows
taller as our bodies shrink.

Mother:

Through all this, Daughter,

let's touch and hold now
when there is little time
for holding.
We will be like moose that rise
clean, as dark water rolls
from their sides.
They become the beating
center of the harsh morning.

Talking with a Window

> *The Five Sisters Window in York Minster*
> *is figureless dark glass stabbed by red slashes.*

If god appeared to me
what would she be like?

> *A womb*

Would she look like you
women of the window –
a black sea of roots that twist
over shafts of sapphire
scattered like poppies in the field?

> *And like you.*
> *Your unborn children*
> *cry to come out.*
> *The light sends them*
> *scurrying back inside.*

Bless me, then, for I have sinned.

> *And I will bless you*
> *for you will sin again.*

But I can't connect the two
the blessing and the sin.
I'm afraid of dying alone.
"You have ruined your life,"
scrawled on the walls of my room.

> *That's not god's voice.*
> *She's big enough, your god,*
> *for both, the blessing and the sin.*

You mirror the sleeping dream in me
that sits up, shouts from my eyes.
The fearful church should camouflage
your spill of blood and longing.

> *It is your story I tell.*
> *Guard your own night,*
> *teeming a fragile as it is.*

From

Green Journey, Red Bird

Birches

They remind me of walking young
and alone through the cloister door
down the long tiled aisle in white,
then at the altar – the pull of my hair being cut.

I thought I had married god
holding nothing but air in my thin arms.
On hands and knees, my mouth pressed
to the floor, I felt invisible.

Years ago I walked out the heavy locked door
but the cloister followed me or I followed
the quiet hallways until it seems
that I've come back with arms held wide
but empty still. The first time was practice
for this season when women become invisible.

Men's eyes look through me now
as April morning sunlight slides down the length
of eastward facing trunks,
half of them wedded to light, half still in shadow,

like the egrets I saw last autumn, their bodies
punctuating a black pond, their reflections rooted
as if stillness were their one desire.

How to do the Ropes Course

1 Look Up

From here on the North Shore
everything flows downward
as wild rivers tumble and crash
their path to Lake Superior.

You and I are changing –
one downward step, then another
until we stand in a new landscape
with ice going out, booming and we,
disoriented, bemused, all senses open
to the roaring of it.

First we climb and balance; then we fall.
The body starts to dry.
The moment of greatest pleasure
 becomes movement without sound,
 like watching dancers from a distance.

2 Put On The Harness

You are gone
like a word I know I have
but can't find –
drifting note
smear of apple skin
empty chair.

Later as I walk into the room
looking for something else I lost,
the gladiola waves like a magenta flag

and you are waiting.
Old friend, you say,
why did you worry?

3 Put One Foot In Front of the Other on the Balance Beam in the Trees

It is like the time we lay
in the grass below stars, listening.
The adagietto was a wall
or a blue doorway in the wall,
the long road into north,
fire road that climbs between pines
then drops into silence behind silence.

The shadows behind trees becoming
your hands – I remember stars spinning
and your hands behind them.

4 Jump Far From What We Are Losing

Most people stand on the platform
and leap. I sit on the edge
and squirm off feeling the wood
grind beneath me .

Something in you wants
to know the truth about the world.

When we walked along the sand,
your body had the feel of a running horse.
Now you leave like water leaves
memories in debris on the shore.

Check harness. Close eyes. Push.
Between us the air, jagged.

A Little Helper

That's what my mother wanted.
It was hot work. She wore print dresses
and told me to iron while my brothers ran
to the river with BB guns and hunting knives.
Their shirts, rolled like sausages, waited, damp
until the iron flattened them.

One week of shirts for five men,
iron, brick heavy, sprinkle
the water bottle, slap it down,
push steam ahead of it, travel
those wide cotton backs,
do the yokes without wrinkling,
the narrow sleeves.

The day her brother, Patrick, fell at work
Mother asked me to iron while she waited
at his bed. I dug through the pile for
the easiest shirts, then ran to the beach.

When her brother died
I drowned in her rage
over the ironing undone, the daughter
who was never a help, or helper –
our unspoken loneliness as my brothers
slammed the door on their way in and out again.

Red Bird in Winter

A winter wind blasts from the Mississippi
past caves and oil tanks, over train tracks
then down West Seventh where it batters
the girl who walks with ice-crusted scarf
bruising her mouth. Beneath a uniform skirt,
leggings her mother makes her wear.
These she removes and hides carefully
in the bushes behind the bowling alley.

She passes the bar then Nedved's florist.
Ahead, Schmidt's brewery sign flashes
a staccato that stays in her striding bones,
always cold, wrapped in layers, hiding bones.
Her mind churns with voices. Her mother warns:
Stay away from the river; it's dangerous for girls.

Get in the car and help me find Highland Park,
the man says. Voices of nuns push her feet
as she runs, *stay pure stay pure*,
runs with guilt in her frightened, Irish bones.

She runs through the stacks of the library.
From the tall clerestory window where the sun
is always going down, she reads the ice
encased river snaking southward.
The dwindling light, spare, unforgiving, is her own.
Frozen there, the chinks in her heart stuffed
with feathers, she imagines a Fra Angelico lazuli,
feels eternity as her heart, that hungry cardinal,
beats on in its cage of bone.

River Cop

For my brothers

The department didn't know what to do
with his large hands and deep angers,
so they gave him a boat and the river to patrol –
uncharted territories, nude swimmers, drunken boaters,
and rope swings to cut down every night.

They were startled by his zeal, the parade
of nude boys, each day's catch shivering in blankets
because he hid their clothes. Mother rode the bus
down to the station to claim my speechless brothers.

The Mississippi cut through sandstone cliffs,
wild bottoms of old St. Paul – the river cop's boat
a moving target as he chugged up and downriver
waving his gun, threatening to shoot stray dogs, swimmers,
hunters down every day to check their traps.

From the shelter of the river caves, boys stoned his boat,
but when they saw the river cop, who couldn't swim,
floundering in deep water, they rescued him.

One summer night, Bill and Jerry dragged
a small civil war canon all the way to the caves
below Otto Street where they loaded nuts and bolts.
Soon metal struck the river cop's boat, a hollow clang
echoing through the river chamber, shaking tumblers,
beer bottles off the shelves of West Seventh Street bars.

Sirens filled the streets, but police refused to chase
kids into caves where in the dark, under garlands of bats,
they toasted a new street legend.

Boys who would soon die in Vietnam
broke free of cramped houses, tiny yards –
never naming the violence that cut sweet and murky
as the Mississippi through their street lives.

Heron

In two hours the fog-bound night heron
has not moved from the neighbor's roof,
its snake neck and beak stretched
as if fishing in air,
each mottled feather visible
on a tweedy breast facing north.

Could be a kind of goodbye,
the same as I feel these days.
Could be blessing the house
where a young couple wait
for a child to arrive.

Could be trying to see its own brightness
the way a mother studies her child,
the angel's awed-by-her-beauty look
in Donatello's annunciation,
all surprised tenderness, the virgin.

Could be wanting a message
like the call from my son in L.A.
After filming a birth he wants to thank me
for having him, calls me a perfect parent,
but I know the failures.
I count them leaf by plunging leaf.

Here where the cold wind sends birds
hurling themselves over lakes
in long strings of sentences,
the heron has waited too long.
Stay, risk the cold, I want to say
but I can't promise anything, not even
attention enough

to keep the grey body from lifting
into a sky, suddenly bereft.

Michaelangelo saw the end of it
as his Pieta emerged from stone.
He carved that pain into the mother's face.

Symbiosis

There are spaces in old trees
that open into other lives.
Spotted choral orchids
live on fungi at their roots
almost but not quite parasitic –
after flowering their tiny capsules nod.

Is it like that in me – almost benign?
A partial eclipse is seen as blood on the moon.

Bark buries fire scars in old trees.
In my breast during ultra sound
I see a shape like basalt, eroded in the center.
My mother's scarred body, burns still raw
when cancer killed her. I turn away.
In the coniferous forest, wolf lichen
covers every trunk; cones hang like long fingers
from the sugar pine, heart-wood
a deepest scarlet.

Boatyard, Late October

Plastic wrapped canvas shrouded
empty hulls of yachts and run-abouts
beached on trailers,
strewn all over the dusty lot.
We come last each year
pulling the smallest boat,
hoarding this heavy piece of summer
as long as possible.
It still echoes our noisy lovemaking
and the hollow slap of waves.

Around us, now, autumn fields burn
a low chocolate before rotting brown.
Now I wish for the dark boats
moving slowly in the night;
want back the light barges
gliding silently to nowhere;
wish for the docks in summer
places where what can't happen happens
where decisions are strung out
in the fine air between leaving and staying.

When I walk uphill toward home
part of me stays on the shore
fallen into the possibilities of going.
Like my Celtic grandmothers
I wait always for boats to return
dragging green promises, never kept.

Night Birds

A night heron, head inclined, freezes, eyes intent.

Nothing gentle in this night bird who brings silence
to the pond, stops the laughing red-wing blackbirds
feeding among stones, ends jay's ululations – silence
from distant shores worn in her deep shimmer.

She turns away from me in her white gown and veil.
Old nun, round shouldered at prayer, she lifts her wings,
stares into tree visions, disappears in blue reflection.

All my life I've known these old women praying.
Now I'm one of them. Crone dreams I never wanted
live in the hollow oak outside my door.

I hear their shadow-voices, collect their spells
and verses, trade one night with its cloak
of threaded silver for another.

From

The Illuminations

Histories

When I read my mother's writing
I hear her, see her hand shaking.

I am my own collector, docent
telling my survival, my subject,

the past looms while the future
shrinks on parchment scraps.

Give me books I can see and hear
at the same time:

the Rabula gospel, the Lindisfarne,
a copy of the Qur'an, a Buddhist folding book.

Let me read the way a child
reads a picture book,

a kind of eating
urging me to utterance,

a reading of the body,
the holy words, the world.

In the Margins of the Pages
Inspired by the Book of Kells, Trinity College, Dublin

1

Illumination

It is March 19, feast of St. Joseph;
the *Book of Kells* is open to St. John.
His eyes, bottomless, now blue, now green
engulf me as when I walked into the Mormon Center,
saw that giant Jesus on the ceiling.
I wanted to fall face to the floor, wanted to believe it all.
The whole creed of it. The repent and follow of it.
The flesh and blood and bread of it.
I do and its opposite. Like that Celtic painter
in the tower, I hold in my mind two thinks at a time.

The lion god on every page
reviver of cubs, swallower of sinners:
we with our heads in its mouth.

2

God is in the Scribblings

Kells Monastery, 800 A.D.
Summer Winter
the monk writes
in a stone tower
that shuts out both Viking
and rain-washed air.

He transcribes holy words
onto calfskin – it's the doodling
that keeps him going.
His pagan hand draws wildly
in colors he creates

painting lizards kermes
from the bodies of pregnant insects,
giving "A" a crown of gold
filling the curve of "J"
with birds colored from verdigris,
folium, woad.

He remakes the heaven he was told.
In his mind stories take sides,
dogs snarl at the cross, mice eat
sacred bread, the snake is watching
limbs of men and women twine.
        It's slow at first
        if a smell, the dark root
        if a shape, running
        if a taste, being there
        if a love, finding.

3
Also in the Margins

While the illuminator paints
his sexy dreams,
the scribe complains
about bad conditions
cold, poor light, writes,
Reader, do not find fault
with the script for my arm
is cramped through excess of labor.
My stomach is empty,
my hand shakes.
This too.

4
The Animal Lessons

If you could see the moment

you fuse with what you aren't –
your beginning, your end.
If you could look down on
that cacophony of crows
with the concentration of an owl
eyes rimmed yellow,
you would understand
how the world you see
means something else.

5

Snake

They didn't know what to do with her
those Christian-Pagan men
so they made her snake.
She curls
all over
        their pages
                shedding her skins
                      always returning.
They named her Christ
        in his resurrected body, called her
                the source of all sin, entangled her
                among the letters of this gospel,
                her head in the lion's mouth.

She's that thing within
that changes but does not change.

Once I stepped off a trail
                while hiking the coast path

trying to shortcut to another hill
                and disturbed a nest of snakes.

They scattershot sprayed.
                I jumped back to the path and stayed

thinking of them.
                She's that kind of knowing.

6
Unicorn

Tapestry – A mon seul désir
Let me live in love again
object of my desiring
with the one who loves my
heavy sweetness, my yes,
object of my desiring.

Let my heart be feral
to my own desire.

My days are a river;
my nights discalced.

How fast this
holy terrain
of my wanting.

7
Ecotone

        Zone where species blend
This moment
        this breath
        this time –
        this is what there is.

This serpent
  this wing
  this red pool eye –
  this is what is next.
This bone
  this boat
  this beak –
  one becomes the other
  this is what will be.

And you on this millefleured earth
that sailed, will be sailing
this illumined eye –

this is what you have.

8
She Who Cannot Be Dissected

Her face flies apart
when you look, scatters
like starlings from a tree
then reassembles new.

That's how I see her when
Trinity College Library
displays a model made by
a Renaissance doctor –
a pregnant woman
belly cut away showing
the child inside her
with a man's face –

set between the rows of marble busts
(Newton & Plato & Aristotle &
Hamilton & Demosthenes & Locke.)

Not the calices on the mountain
not the cloud it wears
not the split in the stone
not the new frond
not the ear of the birch
not the footsteps of wine
not the vagina, not the beech
see her grip the earth
see her feet, her feet

9

Around the Edges of the Pages, Curves and Coils

Trinity knots and Celtic coils
women like the interlaced foliage
a face caught there.

At the Glastonbury well
a woman bends to fill her jars
with water that flows
from spring to well to spigot –
a lion's mouth.

The water flows
into bowls that look
like uterus, fruit halves
through a labial opening
to more bowls
beneath and beneath,
then onto a flower
or phallus, then
into a garden pool.

Her smile dazzles in her dark face.
I drink and wash.
Mother, I want to say, *I'm ready now.*

Walking in the woods, I saw
birches looping and bending
and more than birch,
around one tree, a numinous
light that my eyes missed
in their brief soundings.
And so are we, ourselves and more.

Let me touch you Lady.
You are in the margins of the pages,
and so am I.

10
Beginnings

Ahead the mountain in all its spring stages –
low band of trembling green,
brown weave of branches not yet budding,
the always pine, the shift and tilt of stony light.
Your whole life is stones shaped from your own dreaming,
from the chorus of voices that come whispering there,
and you have to write the book of your own hours.

Cairns

Inverness, Scotland

1
In the field among cows and sheep
stone age graves marked with standing stones.
No one really knows who the blue-painted Picts were
or what's in these graves appeasing their gods.

2
I set up the tripod and camera, comforted
by its whir and dream myself back.
At first, only the sound of sheep bells distracts
from the feeling of being among ghosts
– until a couple with two children arrive
talking as they scramble over ancient doorways.

3
Echoes spin round me, wind-riven.
When you sink into such a place,
death could come upon you the way it came
to the old Scottish woman
who was resting on a rock in her field.
Death made her part of the field,
of the run-on sentence of snow.

4
Underneath my life
is another life –
between trace and memory
between fragment and completion –
still standing inside me.

Family Stories in London

An Exhibition of Greek Icons

After the spring equinox the sun rising low in the south
shines like a laser through spaces in locust and oak,
strange lights in a burnished city, climbing steps
flecked with gold like those Byzantine icons,
the black architecture visible but not diminishing,
an exhibit of light, *A Conversation With God*.

home

I came carrying stories from the Bangladeshi waiter
in the Afghan restaurant across Marylebone street.
He poured free glasses of wine and thick coffee
and talked of his move to London, now home, how
his parents came for work, want to return, but
stay to be near their grandchildren, how
his wife just arrived, wants to go back to her family.

uneasy

In one icon, the Virgin Hodegetria holds a baby
with a man's face. In another, Mary turns away
from the child; Joseph broods with rounded back.
Angels love each other; only ox breath keeps
the child warm, and cracked gold leaf reveals
a dark and brindled god beneath.

making new

I studied icons and thought of hands
that made them, great forces concentrated there.
Did the holy man fall in love with the woman
as he painted? Did he take brush in hand to touch her
mouth, hips, beneath the folds her breasts,
bowing his head in prayer   painting   desire?

away from

When I hiked Bodmin Moor with my brother
we found stone circles beneath Rough Tor
where families gripped life in the endless rain –
the way ours took root on West Seventh
as the city grew around us.

Streetcars changed to buses. Tail fins, talk of cars
filled our yard and the small house where
we moved away from each other –
he, to the earth's cold edges – Siberia, Alaska;
me, to books, icons, babies.

In the old photo we are toddlers
sitting in front of a garden.
I am teaching him to read
and he looks beyond me
towards the hills and river.

Translations

Lovers look into water, never thinking of Polycrates
who threw a ring into a river for good luck,
and the god sent it back in the mouth of a fish.

A Parisian illuminator painted
Boccaccio's tale but confused
the Italian *anello* with *agnello*
and made a fish with a lamb
in its mouth appear as the Persians
hung Polycrates.

Was it a failure of translation then,
or a failure of meaning?
Either way, Polycrates was killed.
Did he betray himself, believing
in symbols that didn't work?

Take the letters carved
on a stone tablet that I touched
in that small museum at Epidaurus.

The spiral Mycenaean script could be
a record of business or judgment or irony,
the story of a murder by twins, how one
was punished and one went free.

The spiral script could be a love poem,
words that come close to what they mean,
could say love smells of oregano, is an owl in the night,
or love gives six gold coins, a bolt of filtered cloth,
is luck, is lapis, basil, a fish with a lamb in its mouth.

The Name of Destination

*On flying with two hundred Hmong people
migrating from a refugee camp in Thailand*

If the edge has a look, this is it.

The grandmother who can't sit still
opens a plastic bag filled with food,
passes it to young men and women
who hold babies in embroidered carriers,
on their chests and on their backs.

Wearing only the name of their destination
printed on white tags, they remind me
of how my great grandparents held their children
in steerage bunks on a heaving ship out of Ireland.
Eyes dark rings, cheeks sunken, exhausted.

If jumping off happens, it is here.

After landing, a Hmong grandfather fingers
his bundle as he waits at the top of the ramp
for his family, brown eyes shining.
He's wearing pink flip-flops into a cold night
where fatigue, snow and wind await.

If edge has a history, this is it.

The Hmong hill people buried the placenta
in the place where a child was born
hoping to bring her back at the end.

In the Middle

René the van driver teaches us some Spanish,
says, *La mitad la naranja,* meaning half an orange,
also meaning, my spouse, my other half.
He wants us to stop halfway between
Panajachel and Antigua to shop at Paulina's,
a trap for tourists where we buy serapes
that we will never wear in public, but they bring us
the comfort of the sixties.
We know sweet René gets a cut from the sale.
"The blue is good for you," he tells me.
The orange he holds up for Suzanne.

> *Seeing the beauty, learning to see*
> *the world in which it lives*

My mother used to say,
"See how the other half lives,"
meaning those who are not poor.
Now, mother, I live in the other half
but I am finding it's no half –
only the tiniest tip of the orange
and all the rest are poor.
I like having money.
Can you tell me how to live my life?

> *I am searching for "la mitad,"*
> *the middle ground of guilt*

At sixteen, I worked part time
at the dime store with Rosita,
who worked full time in yard goods,
all day cutting and measuring cloth.
I went to her house to play cards

in the West Side neighborhood,
poorer than mine on Seventh Street.
Her husband swore in every sentence,
Jesus and Jesus and Jesus.

René is a teacher
But makes more driving for tourists –
one thousand quetzals a month.
He gives us conjugations.

When I ask, "What is a llano?"
he thinks I mean "yawn"
and we conjugate for *yawning*
yo bastizo, ella bosteze, nosotros bostezamos.

> *Seeking a way to be closer to the world*
> *and be less a part of it*

I wanted to be like Jesus,
was already poor, had nothing
to give away so joined the convent,
made a vow to own nothing.
Even the toothbrush was "ours."
We were given two habits to wear,
but we were not hungry.
Poverty was the easiest vow.

> *Searching for "la mitad"*
> *the middle ground of guilt*

A gift to visit the home of Zoila,
a weaver in her Mayan village.
She shows us how to make tortillas
over the open fire and eat them hot and fresh.
When we walk up mountain with the girls —

Lilian Maribel, Astri Sofilia and Arelisa –
they show us fields of squash, cilantro, beans.
We see farmers working on such steep fields.
They're tied to stakes so they won't fall.
Boys come down the path, wood on their backs,
Buenas tardes, buenas tardes.
Later, the girls sit at Zoila's new table
and read to each other in the fading light.

>   *Seeking a way to be closer to the world*
>   *and be less a part of it*

When I was a young woman,
I wanted to come to Guatemala
to teach in the mountains
in my black veil and heavy shoes.
When I left the convent, I said
I'd never again wear those black shoes,

but here I am, walking in my time,
"the last half," walking the cobbled streets
of La Antigua wearing nun shoes
on my sore feet, the learner not the teacher.
I am watching the hands of weavers,
trying to reach them as they move
red and orange across their looms.

>   *Seeing the beauty, learning to see*
>   *the world in which it lives*

A History of Rain

My mother taught me
wringer and washboard,
how rainwater is best for hair,
and to soak clothes covered
in mud from a grassless yard.

Outside the kitchen door,
she collected it in tubs,
added a little lemon juice.
After scrubbing I helped her push
my brothers' cotton shirts and pants
through the wringer, swaying
to the water's swish.

I understand women who study
the science of keeping children clean.
The children I meet on the dirt path
in San Antonio Aquas Calientes
shine in rain-clean clothes.

When I watch the Mayan women add vinegar
to rainwater collected in the town's stone pila,
I think of my mother.

Mud outside our door,
tracked on the kitchen floor,
so much love and anger
in her long history of work.

La Azotea: *A Rising Wind*

This is the year for lavender in Guatemala.
Jacaranda blossoms, like candles lit from inside,
send the eye upward to cloud-drenched volcanos.
Lavender weaves through bougainvillea,
halfway between pink and purple,
each blossom winking its eye.
I watch the way jacaranda might watch over the square,
seeing its own color repeated in weavings for sale by the fountain.

The mothers of San Andreas Ixtapa raised money
so their children could learn a trade. Each table mat
sewn by children who cannot hear or speak
shows one of these petals printed against white
as if it were picked up, kept there,
small light against the dark, sewn on iron machines,
one Singer, five made in China, quiet now.

In my mind the Singer's bobbin chatters
to the lavender dress with puffed sleeves
held between my grandmother's fingers
as she taught me pattern, treadle, warp.
From her, I learned to oil the motor,
but never learned to sew.

Grandmother sewed for me, her favorite, my cousins said.
Musha child, she clucked as she worked – *Musha* because
our names were Mary, because my mother was her first,
because I had four brothers and I was alone.
    Musha child, can't you be still?

It's a lavender light, color the Maya Mary wears
in the church of San Francisco.
If she or my grandmother came to me in the thickest

part of the night, woke me with a flashlight asking,
What do you know? I would say, *nothing* – I know nothing
after so much history, so much work.

Each child takes a place mat to hem,
holds it by the edges as if it were a petal.
I know nothing except wandering and looking up,
pulled by this rising wind of color.

In All Our Fasts

1

Lent in the Cathedral of La Antigua.
Mary is dressed in black robes
trimmed in silver and Spanish lace;
Magdalene wears a nun's robe
with a rope around her waist.

Cinctures of woven rope around waists
meant poverty for the nuns.
Magdalene reminds me
of a short, round teacher from years ago.
Loving Lent, she should have lived in Guatemala,
not in the north's cold regions. *Girls*, she'd intone,
get ready for the fast. Every day for six long weeks,
she'd make us drink milk with spoonsful
of black molasses to keep our young bones strong.

2

When my son asked,
 Are you going to Church?
It's Ash Wednesday.
I answered, *I don't do Lent anymore.*
And I thought,
Why do we celebrate suffering?
You go for me,
you who are searching,
who learned from me.
I'm a traveler of little faith.

3

I remember the priests exhorting us to pray and fast,
but now in Guatemala I wonder,

And what of those who are hungry, forced to fast?
Farmers who can't grow enough beans and squash
in the tiny mountain fields allowed them.

4

Excitement in El Parque Central –
Mary is carried by the strong arms of women
who have fasted to ready themselves.

Below Mary's statue these words:
Benedictaeres Entre Todas Las Mujeres
Blessed are you among all women.

Mary, bless the women, bless all of them –
the round Mayan women of Guatemala
who flatten tortillas over their fires;
who carry their children in *cargadores*
as they weave and murmur and sell.

Bless thin women with face-lifts
drinking cocktails in Santo Domingo,
the old monastery, now a hotel.

Bless me, a woman whose body
expands, who worries about her children –
all children. Bless us in all our fasts.

The World, a Folding Book

The pictures find me.
I don't need the rubricator
who wrote directions on top
of another scribe's work,
telling others how to read it.

Sesame, cumin, oregano
smell of olive and lemon
small boats
with black motors
anchored off shore.

All running together
stone, red dirt
taste of peaches
heat lifting moisture
from my skin.
Everyness of cicada
texture of pthalo blue
the ancient alkahest
connecting
things not words.

We choose the things we love the way
the child draws
what is most loved larger –
two donkeys nuzzling
six goats with bells
stone ring around this lemon tree.

From

What's Left is the Singing

As If

The sky is black with cut-glass beakers
of stars. Everything on the mountainside
is crystal – blades of dried grass,
mouse holes, squirrel nests, pine needles.
With abandon the Milky Way spills out
across the night, so sudden so clear.
As if nothing could ever break,
as if no life could shatter.

This is My Body

When I was a girl I left
my face, my body to find another.
I looked in the church's room of saints.

My body took its cues from these women
with crooked spines, closed eyes,
until I curved and bent my back
under a willow wand neck, the bones
cracking in a leftward lean.

In religion class father Feeney spoke,
white mane halo around his ruddy face,
his fat fingers shaping air.
"Girls, you are growing like this."
His hands forming an hourglass,
his mouth a moue of distaste.

"You must stay pure as the holy mother,
pure as the host at Mass,
pure as the *Hic est corpus meum*
that I say over the bread at Mass.

You have thoughts, words to confess.
You must tell everything.
Confession will save you," he said.

I imagined his heavy flesh under the black,
and looked down my green uniform
at the parts I must keep pure
but his words could not reach me there.
What did he know about my body?
Hic est corpus meum

My own words could save me.
My body was a tongue
with the sweet host upon it.
My body was a stalk,

lily of the valley growing
beside a wooden house,
baby brothers in my arms,
blushing hearts-ease in a pot of clay
beside the shabby door.

My toes in grass,
my fingers turning pages.

My body sang to wood,
to wheels, to weeds
in the empty lot across the street,

to the boys playing Robin Hood
outside my bedroom window –
my face all angles, my body
a glazier's knife whistling on glass,
anticipation, rain on my lips.

Memento

The day before I entered the convent
I wandered the state fair with my boyfriend
in a jagged dream where
bleachers, stands erupted at angles
from steaming concrete streets crowded
with teens nuzzling each other.
Those who were going to college,
those who worked at the phone company
pretzled together on the roller coaster.

I didn't understand what freedom was
or how easily it could be given away.
If I had understood then
I would have eaten
two more corn dogs,
spent more time circling
on the carousel,
and on that small boat
through Ye Olde Mill,
given more quick kisses
in the tunnel murk.

I wanted to not be ordinary,
already beyond the familiar,
my heart left and leaving.
I went forth the way loons swim
underwater like arrows, slowly arcing
toward what I thought was freedom.

That night my friend gave me a crucifix
wrapped in a silver bow. He held
it outward, until his arms made
an angled cross in the August heat.

The next day I carefully placed it
on a small dorm bed
surrounded by bleached curtains,
an unlikely memento on my pillow.
This I thought was happiness.
This I thought was love.

Van Cliburn in the Convent

She thought that if she vowed chastity
God would be closer
but one night she sat on the wooden floor
that she had buffed, shined,
her back straight against the cenacle wall
and listened to the young Van Cliburn
play Tchaikovsky's Concerto in D.
She closed her eyes, imagined his fingers
brushing the smooth keys, then felt
his fingers playing her skin.

Inside she heard a wind-aroused river.
You'd have never known it, looking at her
layered in black serge, breast and hair
covered in white linen, wracked by wanting
in the silence that lives beyond music.
The ceiling of the room rose high and white,
her job to dust its fluted corners and tall
windows, velvet draped against the winter.

Outside the cloister, Randolph Avenue
ran downhill to the Mississippi.
She'd come from the bottom of that hill,
had found the river cave with the granite
the boys called Frankenstein's bed.
She danced to Elvis and Jerry Lee
but didn't know this other music.

The last movement crashed
and turned in her.
Moon became night heron,
floes cracked on the river.
Love opened and opened.

That next Saturday night her sisters
lined the long, unlit hallway to chant
and beat their thighs with small chains.
Instead of penance, she dreamed
Van Cliburn. His melodies grew
through walls around her,
becoming her own body song.

The Oak
for Geneice

Your white curtained bed stood
next to mine in the convent dormitory.
We weren't supposed to talk but you motioned
through curtains, pointed to the attic
where we sat on black trunks, stiff
in our new black dresses topped by white collars.
There, surrounded by veils of drying black stockings,
we told our young lives. Yours, a soliloquy onstage
beneath a coruscating moon; my world bounded,
bare as enclosed convent cells.

How one life opens into another, then stops.
What if you had not told a friend to call me
after your cancer spread?
I'd think you were still living in L.A.
healing the sick, finding the needed herb.

The day of your funeral, I stood in an Irish wood,
touched one of the few oaks left by the English
and thought of you, not knowing you had died.
I heard your theater director voice.

The same moment the nuns were praying
at your funeral, I remembered how your hands
shaped air as you told me of Irish shamans
who touched an oak to travel between worlds.
I think you are one of them, you said.
Stop trying to outrun yourself.

When I was eighteen, you tried to push me
beyond myself, told me that we knew each other
in another life, were priestesses in Greece.

I believed everything you said.
Years later I understood.

When I touched the oak, I closed my eyes,
the way you said the old ones did, and saw
a spiral growing from bleached roots, opening, opening.

I knew that I was circling upward on that spiral.
I knew you were there.

One life bleeds into another, then stops,
that boundary marked by trees and rain-shot air.

Parakeet

*The great green greasy Limpopo river
all set about with fever trees. (Kipling)*

Music – African, Jamaican – furrows humid air.
Children chase each other, a parrot swivels
its head, squawks greet the docking boat.

On the ride upriver we watch orange
crowned iguanas, bright ribbons of parakeets
just like those birds I sold as a teenager
in the dime store in downtown St. Paul –
birds that chattered behind my counter
of seed boxes and small mirrors.

Each time I cleaned the cages, one lime green bird
would escape, swoop like a bat through the store,
skim counters stacked with cosmetics,
following its joyful heart.

I climbed after it with a butterfly net,
and daydreamed myself away from there.

Later, I walked into the store a nun,
only my face and hands uncovered.
The manager I'd dated
glanced then looked away.

Invisible, I stopped to visit the parakeets.
My fingers, folded deep in wide serge sleeves,
remembered those tiny heart beats and I still
wanted to fly.

Deeper in the rainforest
toucans flash fire above us,

herons guard the shore.
Tiny, wooden houses sleep in the heat,
while a sloth dangles from a palm branch.

Water slaps the sides of the boat,
insistent as memory,
more precise and more admonishing.

Patterns of Obedience

    1

Obedience is the most important vow.
Just follow our guidance and you will be holy, they said

before they cut her mind
into rough-edged chunks, reordering her
until she became someone who could bow
to say, *as you will*,
who could kneel and ask permission
to speak, to read,
who would fill out a pattern not her own –

like the muskrat, swimming
her one driven trail across black water
as if it were something solid, all day dragging
brown ribbons of weeds from her mouth,
lidless eyes focusing straight ahead,
ahead being all there is, the pond already
freezing at the edges.

Patterns of obedience,
beads on a rosary, cold mathematics
of life lived behind a snow scrim,
held by ice the way it grabs at tires,
clings to gloves, surrounds a soul.

Kneeling, she held up books asking to read
Kristin Lavransdatter, Anna Karenina, L'Etranger.
Each time the Superior, who hated fiction, placed
the book on her own desk, denying permission.

One afternoon a cold wind rustled the cover,
opened a page before her eyes.

Words whispered in that wind telling her
to go forth and read, to never ask again.

    2

Snow flecked her black shawl
as she ran to the college library
into the basement literature stacks.
Her grandmother had knitted it
and she remembered how she told her,
You have to make your own pattern.
Don't just fill one out.

Through low windows
a slow rise of ground to the cloister.
Under a vaulted ceiling of protective oaks,
she just peeked at books at first,
then read, stopping only to copy quotes,
and let words furrow her mind.
Each book, each quote led her
away from the life she was living.

That night a salmon moon
leapt over the tonsured trees,
a rise and fall lamp
in a cracked ice ceiling.

Coming Home

Both natives and visitors in this town
we linger at the windows of new restaurants
remembering barbers, tailors here in the fifties,
the way my father at ninety walked Cathedral hill
telling us stories of the stones.

St. Paul street names are weighty –
explorers, saints and robber barons.
That old man bent over the piano in the pub,
fingers blurring, brings back the revolving piano bar
at the top of the downtown Hilton
where we decided one night to get married
and celebrated by making pilgrimage,
kissing in front of churches, schools, playgrounds
that held our lives on hilltops and hollows of the city.

Starting at the marble block of domed cathedral,
outlined in light, we drove backward in time
down Summit Avenue to the Victorian brownstone
owned by the Christian Brothers
who had just released you back into the world,
then farther west on Summit to Fairview
to the warm sandstone gold of convent on Randolph.
We honored thick doors I'd opened,
head and chest full of clouds.

North on Prior to Nativity, thickset church and school
on top of the hill. Inspired by groomed gardens,
we drove down Randolph to St. James,
humble river parish pressed to earth and shaped
like the bent back of laborers,
where the rag-tag mix of us first generation Americans –
Irish, Italian, Hungarian – learned to read.

Uphill again to our parents' small wood and stucco
houses, each rooted on either side of Snelling.
Our tires carved wedges of snow
toward Minneapolis where the Mississippi curves.
Churches connected the corners of our map
and each churchyard teemed with spirits,
generations of men and women who pushed behind us
shouting many-tongued blessings.

Surfacing

That summer we wore a path
around the lake as if around
a clock whose hands kept time
and us in its tight loop.

Sundays we took the children
in the boat, with coffee and papers,
looking whole to others,
no one knowing how we talked
in circles, grim, accusing.

We watched maples turn,
and lose every leaf,
crushed and broken underfoot.

When fire had dulled again to dun,
when we had seen
each other's hurts perfected,
magnified like barren boughs reflected
upside-down in water, no birds,
except crows, kept their black watch.

The clouds massed, muffled us in snow.
Wordless winter nights each wished
the other gone.

We were digital clocks, numbers flicking
into place, tarnished pennies
in the time bank, a room of months.

With spring we knew, despite the thaw
nothing would grow again from us;
no paths cut through cambered flesh
of clover, wild carrot.

We didn't see white cirrus fingers
drift above us. Didn't know how
love returned to change

the shape of the house we'd made,
unraveling the year of our exile.

Without the help of words, words grew,
welled up as wild honeysuckle
turning clockwise, swaying between us.

Blue Webs

La Antigua, Guatemala

    1
The need in the market surrounds them,
in the middle stall of the middle aisle.
The infant layered as a coffee bean,
    bluish blanket, red fruit
soft folds of red-white, pulp
then crisp white, shell and then
    the bean the infant,
the center called *oro*.

Only one corner of the child's face
visible as it sucks,
the whole head covered by a red woven cap,
for now, well protected from malevolence
this *pequeño del oro*.

The mother smiles, her few teeth showing,
veins in her breast, a breath of blue web
that breast, her arm
the circle almost closed.

    2
If I listen I can hear this mother saying:

See, she's got it now
    finicky one
    she sucks and sucks
    popping like a cork
    from my breast.
There, a sudden jerk
    like the pull of thread
    a dream pulls through her.

See, she is mine
        smelling of warm tortillas
        nursing, clenched fists
        suddenly splay
        like the blossom
        of the pomegranate.

My breasts drain into her mouth
        I feel her belly swell
        my breasts soften
        to the insides of a ripe mango
        a web of heat between us.
See, I slide my nipple
        from her sagging mouth
        thinking to get back to weaving
        my *tapetes* and *huipiles*.

But she sends me a message
        I….. am still here…..don't
        leave…..me.
For now
I can give her what she needs
and I am happy as the milk-filled moon.

    3
Why was it so hard for me?
My mother's voice traveled down
my baby-holding arm.

Poor baby, he's starving.
You should give him formula.
The doctor disapproving,
You're too weak from surgery.
Not enough milk. He needs a bottle.

My mother standing above me:
You can't do it; neither could I.
You're too nervous.

Why was it so hard
with La Leche at the door?

I'm telling you everything is hungry,
inching toward something else.
Who can stand to be separate
from what they love?
When the milk finally came
blossoming through swollen ducts
it was never a gush, never a fountain
but I knew I could do anything.

Beginning with Skin
for Libby

I hold her in ancestral arms:
an ancient Chinese coin
human geometry, heaven's circle
a shoe, a boat in harbor
a light meter counting hopes
a clock, a cipher
a book waiting to be folded
a tongue with the alphabet it cradles
a rattle moving night.

Only what is and the vessel it's in –
a violet yes, in navy blue eyes
Yes, yes I know you.

A prayer bead, a whistle
the clicking of keys
a flare path to follow
through star jessamine,
red valerian, sapphire linen,
curled spiral of fiddlehead fern.

We make a beehive for the infant;
she opens the earth for us.
We are a city regaining its language.

She is our pool, our well.
We listen, gather
her small sounds.

Catch and Release

for Mari

Northern pike are slimy to touch –
two feet of movement,
scaled green radiance
seamed in black
like lead in a tiffany glass.

Thin watery prismatics,
wild rainbows
above the islands
or sunlight on oily streets,
a brush of pink.

We cannot iridesce like this.
There is the gold in Mari's hair.
There is the sheen of love
in her father's eyes,
but our bodies do not shimmer.

A northern pike fights the pulling in,
allows a brief encounter
with Mari's curious eyes,
her quick baby-finger probes.
Thrown back, the fish bolts,
turning purple in that splash.

We turn the boat toward home,
slice through shadows in the channel,
through reflections of pine and birch,
their scents woven into our air.
The baby held in her father's arms
swims away into fish-filled dreams.

And to what did we release the northern?
Who knows its happiness?

Names for Green

In the beginning roar and bloom
apple-skin of sea.

Through trance-light
in the current of timothy grass,
the long emerald bodies of conifers call.

Beneath the cow-hoof greening
wend of morning,
see what was wrinkled, smooth,
what was withered, strong.

We will become what we are –
part fern, part birch
on a Picasso earth,
a simultaneity of greens.

An onslaught – always one more
hill dotted with lambs, wool tufts
poking though a comforter.

And in between,
wind-noise of naming.

Let me hold you then in sage,
stem and stamen.

We will enter the brief
cloister of Cistercian night,
single-note moss like a moon tasting.
All of it light.

What's Left is the Singing

The first time I walked into that red
gallery, Van Gogh's iris leapt
from the wall. *There*, I thought, *is God*.

A single chant blossoming into polyphony,
one bulb unfolds snakes that writhe
into a music not human.

The keening heart ascends
from choral rhizomes, dirt, armfuls
of water, violet, deep Chartre blue,
and forges a psalter on canvas.

Fleur-de-lis, iridescent blue
of butterfly wings, released
voice beyond festival and praise,
that smoky sound of life rising
through sword-shaped leaves.

The iris leans to the left as if
pushed by insistent wind.
Fierce love burns each bloom
until it vanishes.

From

The Lifeline Trembles

Wounded Angel

Too many spires –
more bells than she had feathers.

Warm-hearted sins, wearing crimson dresses
in blazing gardens, waved her in.

She shed radiance – the grace
a folded white robe at her breast.

Nude, alone as rain
many sleepless eyes on her body –
she thought on his desire.

Like the bleating wave tracing the line of foam,
she wanted to touch those fringes
of soul on his skin.

Everything moving up from trees ensured
earthiness of the heart,
a direct speaking from wounds.

Moon-like blades unlocked
the daily bread window.

She heard a roar of wings, her mind's body
ran through acres of time and wheat

until she fell, her bee hive flesh
sheltering one holy thing –

a red-tipped feather from her unfinished
leave-taking wings.

Ars Poetica

After Jackson Wheeler

Because my mother's mother carried her Irish language
across a stormy Atlantic to St. Paul

Because my great grandfather who lived to be 100
sang in Irish as he bounced us on his bony leg

Because on the front porch of my grandmother's house
the cousins, all named Mary, learned 100 names for green
from rebel songs

Because I lived sixty years before I learned my mother's father
died drunk under the hooves of a horse he was driving

Because my cousin, Sheriff O'Connor, who took bribes
from Chicago gangsters, gave money to my widowed grandmother

Because when I read about him in St. Paul histories
I thought saint not sinner

Because my father's tiny mother came from Galway
with a family too full of priests and nuns

Because she loved to talk in the way of Irish women
over tea and toast at small tables

Because I grew up in the quotidian music of women's murmuring

Because men were either silent or overbearing
I learned my life with *Ann of Green Gables* and *Little Women*

The bus plying the Old Fort Road to school
became my Bridge at San Luis Rey

Because art and music were in the church
I thought beauty belonged to God

Because roots of my young astonishment
cling to my inner life like the pine cone –
growing, even after fire, living scales

Because in the convent we were told to be silent
I picked up a pen

Because of my heart's homelessness

Because a poem waits for me to see it
the way Monet's last painting
his exact pink and red primroses
waited for his uncurtained vision

Because my granddaughters
listen to my tales of trolls and beanstalks,
their eyes pools where words sink and grow,
the way I once listened to the old ones

Because words unwrite as they are written
un-speak as they are spoken

Because love will not let go
I do not want to die without writing
my unwritten watery universe.

Lost: A Sister's Tale

Adapted from the Grimms' tale, "The Seven Ravens"

Four black hawks circle the freeway at twilight
like the four lost brothers of a girl
walking across the fields

carrying her mother's ring tied to a handkerchief
a wooden stool, a loaf of bread
a pitcher of water to ease thirst.

So hard to keep an eye on her
stumbling through fallow fields, overgrown forests
even her brothers lose sight of her.

They beat their wings
cry their hoarse signal *kri-i, kri-i*

sister, sister in dark syllables
during their hunting hour

when rabbits and voles browse
the rustling grass and bits of violet cloud
break off to drift over eastern mountains.

They hover above and you
crane your neck as the sky
sucks you into blue

so high you forget where that girl was born,
in what century, country, village,
what your name was,

the taste of your mother's bread, and this
longing that swallows all others.

The oldest brother breaks the circle
heading east and pulls the others, weaving
black and gold behind them.

Do they spot you, or some
crooked branch, twitching shadow?

Stygian wings streak the vineyard kingdom
of crows into blue hills and you wonder

if you'll reach the edge of the world
to enter the cavern
where hawk brothers sleep.

If you'll have time for a sip of wine
from each of four beakers, time to slip
your mother's ring into the last of them.

In which country has she left
her cumbersome stool, where is your cup?

When four hawks cleave the evening sky
and disappear, the air vibrates with leave-taking.

Gardens of Paris

    1

At the Rue de Varenne, Rodin's thinker
rules the rose garden,
his bronze thoughts lost to you and me.
He appears again, brooding
above the last judgment doors:
Abandon hope, all ye who enter.

Carved beneath him, eternity's lovers
twist in the embrace of the damned,
to yearn but never touch,
lovers who grasp for each other
even as demons drag them to the fire.

A blackbird sings his searching song
as we walk under budding plane trees
in our aging bodies where desire
simmers after all these years.

Chimney swifts shrill in chorus
diving for insects in the long dusk.
Peonies droop in every triangle of garden
as we cross the plaza behind Notre Dame,
the bridge over the Seine crowded
with spirits – the living licking ice cream
and the dead still hungry.

    2

Tonight the sound-garden
of a Bach concerto drifts from
a medieval church off the Rue St. Jacques.

Silence rises from the Roman dig
at Musée de Cluny.
From rooms of marble statues
rise saints and kings without arms.
The two of us quiet now as the patisserie
at the end of a long day.

We praise the garden of the courtly lover
and the monk's medieval herbs,
fresh as oranges luminous in market stalls.

Praise the short stairway
as we climb to our room.
Praise my heart, still strong.
Praise your body, still whole –
our night's story not yet over.

A rectangle of light spills
through the high window.
I paint you Notre Dame blue.
I am Sainte-Chapelle red. Together,
we're purple in the deep Paris night.

A Beltane Tapestry

Wings flicker as they dip to yarrow,
Monkshood, brambles, meadowsweet,
doves hidden in leaves.

Move back a step and you'll see
a gold thread running through,
one harp chord, the demanding
voice of desire.

Your eye forgets the dancing,
the birds, the piper,
the millefleured world
where a tower floats on a hill,
turrets lost in threadbare clouds.

Shine is all you see.
It glitters, seduces
in this ordered fading world.

Suddenly you tremble inside
a lone poplar welcoming
its finches home.

The Unicorn Tapestry: *A mon seul désir*

I have come back to you, City of Light –
only your colors can save me now.

I'm no longer the mother
of two young boys who ran
from sword to arrow in war museums.

No longer the woman wandering
crypts beneath gothic cathedrals.

At Cluny the white haired lady
holds her jewels to the light
then gives them to the unicorn –
To my one desire.

It's time to give you away now
my chest full of words,
tongue-flood
my one desire –

lark, scent of cardamom,
lilac moon.

Words are the colors I swim.
My heart, the cartographer,
charts to the river, sweeps
back as earth gathers its skin
into pearl, onyx, coral.

I've forgotten more times
than geese cross the morning
how to let go.

What Stone Knows
Dingle, Ireland

These naked fields where one's voice must go
into an orphaned silence, where blackbirds
whistle a challenge to fishing boats.
Where night wanderers, moon loving creatures
seek a crevice of shade.

Autumn air tintinnabulates, as sunlight
caresses the slant of carved symbols
in the Ogham stone.

I trace their lines, hungry for names
as if they were not already deep in me,
words saying what stone knows.

My hands begin to speak at sunrise,
say my hungry heart is a blackbird.
Earth keeps my feet fastened to flesh
but my body like a heliotrope turns –
toward bright red needles, liquid fire,
the composition of light.

From stone walls called lace, blackbirds sing.
The soul is granite cliffs, open sea, island.
We must find our way there.

Palimpsest

If by truth you mean hands
shaping the vertebrae of stars

If by hands you mean oak branches
scratching the moon's face

If by branches you mean that sickle moon
lying on its side as if asking

If by moon you mean pillow, expectant
as we, fingers laced, walk dim streets

If by pillow you mean feather words
the breath of fasting lovers

If by words you mean answers
where the moon tilts on its side
like a burning blade

If by answers you mean bruised trees,
clouds, lights of a far-off city, or the way
your finger slides into my closed fist

trembling the lifeline, or the way
your palms resurrect my breasts

California Morning Song

Olive tree bent on the hill,
bathed in expectancy.
Lavender and white stone.

Sea wind turns the world transparent.

Jade shell
Pink Perfection camellia,
water-cuts in sand

mutate on the zigzag border
between wholeness and coming undone.

The horizon a gold line,
broken by tankers and tall ships,
between visible and unseen.

How loneliness ends
though you are far from home.

How a sailor becomes
the oceans she sails across.

Both Ways

In dingy schools, cramped rooms –
elms beating at the windows,
rain dictating its own orthography –
they gripped crumbling chalk
in fingers black with ink.
They fed wide-open minds
to calm our hungry turbulence.

In my chaotic girlhood I followed
outmoded women in black –
so much like myself
and completely other.

What was it, the mystery
beneath black serge, nylon veil,
linen wimple, gimp over the breast?
Only face and hands available
to my curious eyes.

Now, when I stand in front of my class,
nuns gaze at me from the back of the room,
shake their heads, disapprove,
correct my mistakes
with the truculence of the dead.

Sometimes, only their names
wind paths in the wood of the pews.
Margaret, Clare, Mary Honor
still climb wooden steps
to tiny rooms or kneel in chapel.

I hear the voice of their exhaustion,
see the emptiness which hid
the shining core of their lives.

The Poet Goes Fishing

In memory of poet, Joyce Uhlir

When the tip of your rod
scribbles on air like a toddler's crayon

and the length of nervous fiberglass
bends to the pull of weed or pike

you struggle to your feet, most in love
with this questing.

When it first comes into view,
that mute silver flash

wends its way through
wavering fields of water.

Now when it could be fish
or angel

you stand, straining to hold
that almost cracking rod

like Abraham to God, crying out,
Here I am

as the surface fractures, showering light.

Between Rivers
for Sylvie

Tell us, Orion, great hunter
while you pace our land,
where can we anchor the tents
of our many languages, our longings?
Who will hear us through the din
of so many singing tongues?

The moon crosses a black sky
thick with shrieks of hawk, crow, owl,
with words I've forgotten.
Buried dialects, whole alphabets
on the far side of rivers

crowd my mouth, adding weight
and grit to what can only sing.
A slow Irish rolls from my tongue
to my tiny, dark-haired granddaughter.

From her eyes, somewhere between
the depths of the Nile, the Rhine
and the verdant marshlands of the Shannon,
a question drifts through the reeds –
Where am I?

Here, child, is your home, your mother tongue.
To those who crossed borders, who entered
harbors to make it yours, *thank you*.
Orion will follow you, child, watching over
all the cities where you will live
all the landscapes you will love.

Field Walking in County Donegal

I stumbled upon a fairy fort –
a sacred circle of large stones.
The wind is a sea surge
in a holly tree.
It's peacock-tail crown
has turned it from a bramble hedge
to an emerald and amber,
soon to be flaming, bowl
of mysteries and whispers.

Sky a frosted pane, a tumble of crows.
Fox-red bracken feathered
chocolate rabbit holes.

I turned around inside the circle
three times, sun-wise
as my grandmother said.
Nothing happened.

Climbing high, stony Marmore Pass,
I stopped at the shrine of St. Columba,
paper prayers flapping in wind,
wilted flowers in jars; then I found
the holy well, glint of dropped coins.

I gazed down on the field
the stones, the fairy tree, the sea
rapt in salty concentration,
and I wondered if the world
could ever be changed
by shambling, ancient love.

Istanbul Winged

Indigo islands raise up a city of merchants
stringing bridges, erecting a palace
hermetic as a jewel box.

The sky spreads, indifferent,
across layered history, unloading
a sparse cargo of summer clouds.

By late afternoon, the last boat
to the Black Sea slips
gracefully out of the harbor

where small dolphins leap
between ferries and black tankers –
liquid turquoise.

Tonight seventy ships line up
begging berth in Istanbul port.

A shuffling man brings roasted lamb wrapped
in newsprint through the darkening alley –

sky brewed to the hue of smoked tea
haunted by flame,
stars like sparks in a somnolent brazier.

Prayers, call and response from giant mosques
echo among ancient, humble buildings.
A holy tree here, a goddess, I once knelt to.

Painted-over mosaics and frescoes
bleed like silver moonlight
through thin white clouds.

Aging in Ephesus

In a tea garden,
four small tables with chairs, I hear
the clamor of motorbikes muffled
by trees and simplicity of ruins.

The friendly innkeeper pours wine and tea
served with small silver spoons.
All time gathered in this quiet,
grey and white kittens winding around my legs.
Next to me, a column from the temple of Artemis.
On the hill above, ruins and the tomb of St. John.

Storks, gulls, soft conversation –
even as the call for prayer resounds
from every roof top – kingdom of stone paths,
ruins, dirt, wild hollyhocks and kittens' mewling.

With satellites surveilling above me, I see
how nothing and everything changes,
how marble survives violent sun,
wind hissing in stone crevices.

When a whole fish, grilled, dressed with tomatoes
and cumin, appears on a plate, *I want to kiss it.*

From

Cypher Garden

The Open Window
Nice, France

Through shutters, an open air market
where a juggler tosses oranges,
fist sized peaches into shoppers' hungry bags,
loving the torrent of his own talk.
Women in line vie for his attention, roll their eyes
when an old one pushes to the front.

Slabs of salmon bake on terra cotta bricks,
peach and melon, slashes of mustard and olive.
Fish sleep in ice beds, eyes pasted black spots.
In black pots peppers sizzle and burn.
Everyone carries a brown loaf,
each pockmarked crust, the caul of a miniature monk,
as the horizon runs with raspberry juice.

The walls of our room are cool and white.
Lunch pulls us to the table –
burnt tapenade and a pastry puff,
with pureed cod and fraise,
grilled shrimp, aubergine with red sauce.
The outside world clatters
beneath an edible, steaming sun.
Rhubarb compote, vanilla glace for dessert.

White sheets warm the bed.
From the window light streams
through our bodies.

Cypher Garden

St. Olav Cathedral, Trondheim

1

On the flagstone floor
a carved garden dedicated to the deadly sins.
Each sin signed by an animal
an inverse sky of bestial constellations.

Gluttonous fat pig, low to the ground,
razor clawed crab secreting anger,
sweet sloth loving total laziness.
Empty squares demand sinners lay down
each transgression, stamped upon.

2

Whoever made animals emblems of sin?
I tried but couldn't think of deeds
in my long life I would quash.
My commitment to appetite,
crème brulee, provençal wine,
a bouillabaise of taste and smell?
Finding sun, my home of slow dreams?
Butterflies connect the patchwork
of my anger, soaring into the spheres,
pigments from the warm body of the earth.

3

The animals in my cypher garden
fly in Chagall's vision, at the center of all things,
red whirling in a womb of yellow,
dancing bull and cow, flying fish, firebird,
Adam and Eve laughing
as they are expelled by a tender angel
flying out of and into hope.

4
I was twenty-six when I left the convent,
not knowing how my clumsy body could rise,
then fall like a feeding pelican, guttural moaning
in blue backed, red rimmed ecstasy.

Was it a sin, I asked a priest?
I don't know, he said.

5
Too many years before I flew into my body.
I would stamp on that sorrow –
its cypher was a blank slate.
What came after floods the margins.
Emblems in lapis, in carnelian.
Colors in the language of cardinals.

Think of the statue of the black bear
nosing a berry bush at the entrance
to Madrid's Puerto del Sol.
I was that beary appetite
and the sweet fruited bush.
I was so hungry.

Haiku Ladder

Haiku saves lives – Sonia Sanchez

It gets inside you
deep like the blues, and deeper,
a river rising.

I was a young nun.
My mind hiked through syllables
beast hungry for words.

I could buy one book.
My twentieth year Basho
fell like a ripe plum

into my desperate hands.
His poems mirrored my mind.
I came alive with them.

I grew Haiku eyes.
The short lines slipped from my hand
flew into the world.

May evening shower
petals from the wild rose bush
moon-light on the ground.

My thrown rock became
Basho's frog plopping lidless
into convent pond.

Water rings exploded
silver dancers leapt shoreward.
Inside and outside

green growing wood weeds
covered the eyes of the priests
Recall you are dust…

The winter white pine
gives ice a place to hang on.
Haiku saved me.

Season of the Swan

The doe hesitates behind trees,
steps into snow filled meadow.
I could take a bucket, fill it
with the tracks of her small hooves.

Touching an oak, I become an oak.
Watching a deer, I become a deer
walking across to the saltlick.
If I watch deer drink,
I am the tang on their tongues.

Once I drank from a clean
northern river, tasting granite,
moss, moose, a trace of rabbit,
grouse, the prints of weasel and quail.
As sun broke over rock
mountains melted and rivered
in my mouth.

You waded up the river,
knew the piney silence
of green forests,
skipped a stone, watched the circles
lave and loop and spend.

Now we wash our hands,
break the bread
and lift our cups
to the canopy of leaves.

I want to call you,
lick water from your hands
but I can't say your name.
Reach with me into night.

On the narrow bed I think of our first night.
Beneath your hands, I became a brook,
your tongue on pebbles.
Now we are swans.
We close our eyes and dive.

Remembering Paris: A Poem Sequence

White Nights

When you remember me, conjure Paris,
the clack of red high heels
in the night courtyard below our spiraled stairs.

You won't remember what I wore,
red dress with blue sash.
I remember your French,
voice warm, like a balm,
your eyes, that deep end blue
color playing zither on my heart.
I saw the sea in them,
grace light of sun on waves
the shores we would follow.

Night after light filled night, we walked
along the Seine with our children.
Timothy talked beside us.
Andrew ran ahead scouting for *glâce*.
Later, in the small apartment bed
I lay with my head on your chest.
Even now, some savor of me wanders
narrow Paris lanes
clinging to those aureate nights.

Meditation in Notre Dame Cathedral

Before us
  Behind us

You are the one who calls the women
to this dark church.

You, scarlet footsteps of setting sun
moving up dark columns
inside Notre Dame, that great womb.

You carry our sorrows –
the sorrow of women whose babies died,
women whose mothers died in childbirth,
whose men went to war,
whose men beat them,
women who couldn't read or write,
women who wrote in secret,
women who could not own,
who were owned.

Women who watched history written,
whose ideas men took and turned into law
or poetry, sojourners from far places
who never saw home again,
who nursed babies on bunks in the deep hold,
women who lost their own language,
forced to speak another's,
women who invented tongues and songs,
who sang the songs to children,
women who prayed, who cursed,
who were stoned.

We bless them as they pass through us.
We shout their dark sorrows.

Lady in the cathedral
Voices in the dark
Teach me to listen.

Carrying a Green Branch

When you remember me, speak of that French summer.
Talk of Andrew, Carlos and Bernardino
in the stone courtyard, speaking the language of *boules*.
I'm good at telling them what I mean,
my son says, his bright eyes dancing,
showing how he hits an imaginary ball.
They like to play war, like us, but they don't call it war.
All afternoon the thump of rubber on stone.
Outside the heavy courtyard door, traffic roars.
Paris for Andrew is two Spanish boys who throw
balls between the iron railings of his balcony –
balls which he must return.

❋ ❋ ❋

When you talk of me, remember Timothy at Cluny,
his mind suddenly able to roam across centuries.
He stops in front of every portrait asking
Was he good or was he bad?
We pore over illuminated manuscripts,
where icons gleam – a world passing
into a world to come, emblems in lapis, in carnelian.
He traces over a crown of gold clasped by two snakes,
a curving arm filled with demons and winged lions.

In a book of hours, we study symbols of the Zodiac.
In my birth month, April,
a peasant carries a green branch to water.
I know I will carry a green branch for Timothy,
a memory – sitting on marble steps
in a hall hung with unicorn tapestries,
naming flowers, fruit, herbs, kings, queens, wars –
names and eras rising from the salty pages of our tongues.

❊ ❊ ❊

At the Invalides a military funeral for French soldiers,
black garbed women cry across the courtyard.
My sons spend all afternoon studying ancient weapons,
the jeweled carvings on swords and battle axes.

They're works of art, Timothy proclaims.
Nowadays, weapons aren't works of art, are they?

At the Grand Palais, crowds worship a painting by Manet.
A young man turns his back on his parents,
rejects the breakfast that his mother made.
On a chair beside him, an ancient sword and helmet,
but the enormous eyes in his marble face
look far beyond the room, past gazing art lovers,
fixed on the clarity of his own death.

I know I'll come back to Paris some day, Timothy says,
if war doesn't come too soon.

Sunflower
    Vincent Van Gogh, 1888

Only a close up of a sunflower
turns to scales of trout or salmon,
ancient patinas or flints of gems,
smell of honey,
rough amber that rises
from strangling vines.

What were you longing for
when you made them?
Tawny flowers, summer wheat,
autumn grapes.

I am guided by color, you said, *by light —*
only they can undo or save me.

Bright yellow burns from inside out
as the sky turns turquoise.
This sunflower stabs me
with a living eye,
makes me see how everything
means something else.
Is somewhere else.

Thundering Up West Seventh

Along the Mississippi, sagging houses,
narrow streets discharge teens
born during the war or just after.
Lilacs droop over sidewalks,
scent the edges of drive-in parking lots.

Saddle shoes crush fallen blossoms,
scarves circle our junior high faces –
bright lips and cheeks, nylon knots
on our chins, badges of sophistication.
We eye the boys in fish tail Chevies,
watch older girls balancing trays –
root beer, burgers, deep fried onions.

In a cloud of greasy vapor, motorcycles roar
up West Seventh from the Harley Davidson shop.
My disbelieving stare trails Cookie and Rose,
their short bleached hair and leather jackets,
arms wrapped around the waists
of favorite bikers while crows in bare oaks
intone, *You can't   You can't.*

One night big Dave offers me a ride.
On his huge black Harley, my long braid flying
in that joyous wind, I cling to him
senses open like mouths, shouting *Yes!*

Yes! to the long tongue of the road
lolling out before me.
Yes! to West Seventh transformed to ridge
across hills, shining Agean below.
Yes! to a white trail up mountains
where moose dance through drifts of snow.

Yes! to the clouds blooming lavender.
Yes! to grand bazaars and cobbled streets.
No! to staying home, my mother's anger,
my brothers' fights.
My pulse like a stadium of fists
punching *Yes! Yes! Yes!*

Later, I walk with Kathy and Sharon
past dark, crowded bars
ankle deep in tenderness and lilacs,
the roar of Harleys in my blood.

By Way of Words

Locked within the radiant metal skin
of a DC 10, in flight from one life
to another, I stare out a scratched
porthole to my Midwest,
twilight coming on.

Below, through miles of cloudless air,
a freeway cloverleaf glitters, a brooch.
Sweet planet of my youth,
my childhood.

From the memory room of my brain,
Seamus Heaney's voice lilts:
You are neither here nor there,
A hurry through which known and strange things pass...

I am a vessel of music,
assigned to Seat 11A, moving
mid to west above the continent
in the vacant space once called God's.

The flight attendant comes by for trash
and Eliot intones in my head:
Because these wings are no longer wings to fly
But merely vans to beat the air...

The captain's voice announces our descent.
I turn back to my fertile window.
Teach us to care and not to care...

First the desert of small LA house tracts,
then the light studded spines of buildings
slowly rise into view.

I think Emily here – her *certain slant*
waiting traffic stalled at salt rimmed lights,
tiny boats and rising lace-fringed sea swells.
Like Neruda I want *to be,*
and be nothing but light in the dark.

Praise

I want to praise what cannot last –
scarlet and orange leaves
crushed and trampled, the way
they rise again in wood smoke.

I want to think the way wind thinks,
the way an oak leaf dreams
shadow and light, the way
blackbird builds her nest or a cloud
blooms out of emptiness.

I want to name things
the way the dwarf pine names
shining grubs beneath bark skin,
the way nettles spark fever,
the way tawny owls call feathers
under the new moon
secretly feeding earth and sun.

I tell my hand write like lichen
over stone, a bit of dry rot, a raindrop,
tell my eye imagine like a mirror,
my tongue to speak the mystery of salt.

Speak, but let things be
exactly as they are. How easily
they shelter alone, behind a stone,
how they steal into my ear
and whisper *death, go away*.

The Pleiades turn and return
as night hides us in her black velvet,
little lights, lives setting, rising on earth.

The Gift

In golden midsummer cotton grass
I hunch behind a wind-dwarfed pine
to watch a female moose and her calf
high step from forest to shore.

She lifts her head, long ears twitch
as she inhales inhabitants of a wind
that blows my way so I stay hidden
in my human smell.

Mother and calf bend to drink.
The water, rusty with iron, lies still,
between clumps of reeds.

Liquid rainbows yield to lapping tongues,
flow under velvet to become
marsh light in the eye of the moose.

I see the cotton grass let go.
Gathering, rising – the spirit of each waterhole
deserts its body to ghost over the marsh

like Christ on a church wall ascending.
I know salvation is not the blood of the lamb
but in the blood of a woman when her rivers flow.

In a room golden with morning and moose light
my children emerge from my dark waters.
I give them the river wide after thawing.

Mother Tongue
for Bridget

All you know these early days is calling
mother, father, sister.
Sometimes a bird gurgle of bliss,
a scrap of music –
enough to make cups of your ears.
Words chained in bracelets,
objects, bright and dark –
gifts for your mouth, that temple of new sounds.
Your cries, your moving tongue's wild script.

Your wide eyes search in a green-scape,
for trees, bushes, boundaries blurred
between earth and sky, day and night.
Ahead of you, child, are names
of things and things not yet named.
Ahead of you, mallards and ducklings,
hawks and their chicks.

Inside, you live
all the tender words we give you
so you can make your way
through the glittering world.

From

Nocturnes: Between Flesh and Stone

After Basho

Another year gone
Nun shoes on my feet
Poems in my hand

Illuminator Dreams:

*An eleventh century nun in northern Germany,
scribe and painter*

She copies the gospel
in a tower among oak branches.
She dreams of light
falling across the page,
shining through the leaves,
drawing her in, and she writes
a story beneath the story.

Painting her dream light, she learns
underneath is more.
Too much light to see
in the margins of the world.

With a hard-tipped brush,
she dips into ultramarine
made from crushed lapis lazuli,
paints on calfskin, rests
with the tiny brush in her mouth,
wets it, readying herself
to paint Mary's blue gown.

Her painting, like the scribble
of rain on the lake's wide page,
breaks off light, breaking off
when the light moves on.

She follows deeper, weary
inside the womb of rock, of rain.
She dreams of lapis stones carried
from Afghanistan by merchants
along that great silk road.
Stones worth more than gold.

Once she sat in sunlight
near a waterfall and once
she sang near the southern sea.

This is her story now,
and the light is hers forever.

In a thousand years, another woman will find
flecks of lapis in the nun's stone teeth
nested like tiny blue robin eggs.

Nocturnes

*Joshua Bell plays his transcription
of Chopin, Nocturne #2, Opus 9*

His violin carries me to Paris
where I walk alone in twilit shimmer
as street lamps, bridges shine with rain,
fog rising from the Seine.

The past is a stone in my hand.
I finger it as evening deepens,
plant myself on Pont de la Tournelle,
watch the back of Notre Dame as the sky
shifts through layers of blue.

Darkness shrouds the cathedral.
Even after the great fire,
the flat, dark skeletons of its buttresses fly,
softened by leafing plane trees.

I'm not alone here.
On the bank of the bridge
Sainte Geneviève lays her hands
on the shoulders of a child, a young Paris,
city she once protected from the Huns.

We're not strangers –
at eighteen I was given her name,
aching to become holy Sister Geneviève.

I, who never left St. Paul,
prayed to the protector of Paris
begging her to guide me
on sleepless convent nights.

She looks through sixteen centuries
down on me again,
no longer laboring to be holy.

Joshua Bell's violin distills blue
from Chopin's notes for piano,
the musk of centuries, gathering dusk.
A surge of strings against the night.
Past present future one smooth stone.

Finding Her: Mother Goddess on her Throne – 5750 B.C.
*Statuette in the museum of Anatolian civilizations
from Catalhoyuk (a Neolithic town)*

No more than terra cotta –
warmed earth smell –
her thick body on a little clay throne.
Breasts like large loaves,
buttocks like melons,
flanked on each side
by lion-animals,
her hands, their heads
a melding of woman and beast.

Her taut belly protrudes –
a child's head emerges from between her thighs.
Paleolithic mother goddess, thunder heart
of the earth.

Before Aphrodite, older than Artemis,
her face lifts as she listens to her own music.
Hair piled on her head,
small nose, enduring mouth.

She is walking
through sage, heat, locusts, war.
Her gravity reminds me
of my great grandmother, Johanna,
in an old portrait, black Irish hair coiled,
wine-dark eyes,
body shaped like a hive.

Found whole, surrounded
by ancient fragments of a puzzle,
humming an ancient note.

*Listen,
do you want to hear
all the women resting inside us –
in dirt, rock, chant, darkness?*

I have traveled so far
to find her memory.

Still Life with Lemons, Oranges and a Rose
Francisco de Zurbaran, 1633

Three ripe lemons reflected
in a plate of polished pewter –
breast shaped ovals in morning light,
shadows defined
by slanted autumn sun on stones.

Ancient motifs – the trinity, homages to the virgin –
oranges with blossoms, water in pewter,
the thornless rose, shades of white and tissue pink,
immaculate conception to renaissance viewers.

It's the intensity of color that draws me,
that curls my fists and fingers,
lemony oil, pocked yet smooth skin.
My mouth tightening at the taste.

Round bellied oranges wear deeper shadows,
as do sinners who bite into fruit.

The background, obsidian
color beyond all colors, living pigment
created at the back of the brain,
bright as the history of shadows.
Each color a kaleidoscope
muted with gothic dark.

Roses and Monks: Birmingham, England

Though sometimes as we walk this earth, with the memories of our loved ones shadowing us, we might also become our own holy places: roaming churches, cathedrals and memory mausoleums.
– Edwidge Dandicat

Before sunset, I walk muddy streets,
searching for morning light I missed,
find it in wet flesh of other peoples' roses.

The Pakistani woman at the corner grocery
confides, *I've lived here twenty-five years.*
As soon as my children are settled, I'm leaving
even if my husband stays.
I help her wrap roses – scarlet, coral and yellow –
her own bright colors and she adds,
I miss my mother and sisters.

I ride the train to Shrewsbury,
looking for the monks chanting
on BBC, wanting god-praise
in a cloister trembling with cold.

I find only one large rain-worn stone,
in Cadfael's restored medieval garden
of scurvy grass, hyssop, St. Mary's thistle
citron, cockscomb, apothecary rose.

Going back, I dream the land beside the tracks
is lined with those who've lived before me.
My journey marked by grimy industry,
small back gardens waving laundry,
and graveyards, centuries thrown together –
black stones leaning in chaotic earth.

How can we travel this world without
the dead? We offer roses, granite.

The Songs

For John Berryman

We passed one day on the steps of Lind Hall
you late for class, wild hair, glasses askew.
I was just out of the convent, new in graduate school,
books bouncing on my back as I ran
down Church Street to join the marchers.

Five thousand strong on Washington Avenue they sang,
We Shall Overcome, and then began the chant
that frightened me –
Ho Ho Ho Chi Minh
Ho Chi Minh is gonna win –
I couldn't sing – those jungles
hid my youngest brother.

At home I opened your *Dream Songs*,
blown away by your impertinent piety,
iambic the only verse I knew
until you brought me ear to ear
with a new scripture –
you needled, wheedled me
not with beauty, but scarifying singe
created in all-night drunks,
the blues – your book of revelations.

I wanted some of that wildness in me.
As your songs freed my lines, my fears
your music moved in me,
How could I resist?
I was learning poetry and sex.

Three years later your body hit the rock-hard
waters below the river bridge I walked across.

My brother was in the hospital.
My country was still bombing
Vietnam to kingdom come.

Finding Blue

I look for blue.
— Vincent Van Gogh

I am trying to live each day
as if it were the first,
an Eve waking and naming –
sun a surprise, wing a flash.

Along the pond, just-emerged indigo
dragonflies loop and whir,
wild with sex and the ending
of their two-week adult lives.

Early humans did not name blue.
Did they see it? What did Eve call sky?

I like to think two thousand years ago
a woman swerved off her path to kneel
before a blossom, its color a flutter of sky.
She suddenly named blue, laughing,
bringing others to see.

Now ultramarine and indigo everywhere.
Feathers of hunting jays, the blue fire
of the Côte d'Azure in summer.

Braid in feathers of four wild turkeys
on the roof edge, the youngest afraid to fly.

Flight lessons for young mallards
almost but not quite lifting off, cobalt
flashing from their tails.

Cattails spear an electric sky
where heron drops to the green
swaddle of the pond.

Blue as storm, iridescent, alive
to the rings on the surface
where the turtle rises.

Dragonfly blue rushes through
a quick and private joy.

Vanishing

We live by the mercy of things
no longer with us –
redwings in their swale of reeds.
The waterfall grown small,
creeping its way up the rock face.
Rain-brushed wild roses
hidden in bogs,
pollen buried for eternity.

Wheat in the haze and heat
on its way down the rootstalk.
The ponderous winds
move slowly and sullenly,
the stuff of dreams
while the earth crackles
like peeling canvas
and everything
a human being is made of
sifts in the air.

Dove-blue plums
blown to feather particles.
Grey-white bindweed
crumbles beneath clay
where monarch, starling and lark
are lost for all time.

What will we be when the glaciers are gone?
Flood, echo and fire.
Let us see with an open, wide grief.

The disappeared,
where they were born and died,
shining all around us, the way
burned-out starlight glows
for a time
in the eyes of the living.

Derry in Time of Brexit

I drive through green fields, through the invisible
border fought over again in Brexit,
remembering the English woman's clipped syllables
echoing in the university office in Birmingham,
as everyday rain drummed the windows:
Why would anyone go to Ireland.
They have no history, do they?

Velvet hills hug the fraught city,
pubs filled and buzzing,
hotels unbombed for years now.
The political murals are predictable
but still make me cry,
especially the one of the schoolgirl
who was shot by the British army.

And history's a ditch
for lying in, the Irish say, *if we let*
the gravediggers name us.

My father's father was an Ulsterman,
my mother's father from Limerick.
Walking a line – hard to do
in a cleaved world.

Orange, green, white –
The colors are weapons,
navy blue, deep red.
Tourists choose guides,
either Protestant or Catholic.
Or they take two walking tours,
two clashing cities here.

My father's father, Edward,
converted to marry Nellie from Galway.
He was a rock cleaved open.
Inside the rock, more rock.
An untouchable darkness.
We sat at the feet of his soundlessness.

Storefronts still boarded,
factories defunct, piles
of solid bricks for new construction,
bricks that once smashed windows.

My mother's father, Thomas,
died beneath a horse's hooves
when she was young.
Once horses were weapons of war.
Now they wander in waves of grass,
race on graceful ankles.

Hundreds of years…
One year…
History a river.

There is a peace bridge now,
built by the EU – ending in a park
where British soldiers once bunked.

But marchers still line up
to celebrate William of Orange,
their bright ribbons at odds
with gaunt, angry faces –
wizened like grandfather clocks
that still keep the wrong time.

There's a bell inside this memory

and a hand that rings it.
There's a playground of children,
squeezed between red bricked school
and sandstone church,
lining up by our sizes.
I am always in the front
as we tumble and march
through the doors of classrooms
opening into wainscoted halls.

It's a kind of relief to come in –
jumpers, twirlers, shouters –

for those who played
and those, like me, who played at playing.
For those who watched, walking laps
at the edge of the schoolyard.
We all seemed to float away like leaves.

It's good we are warming our desks again,
such cold little desks
screwed down to the floor.
How good and sleepy we feel
to know what we know.

The young nun will push her veil from her face.
The small hands on the clock will slowly circle,
and the thick brown shoes
we've kept tied all day
will take us home
through streets freshly tarred,
through scraggly empty lots,
lilac bushes, bridal wreath and yards

where grass will not grow,
to our small, crowded houses
fastened firmly to earth.

I remember my great grandfather in his corner,
lost in the smell of drifting pipe tobacco.
Later, the moon hiding from me behind trees,
the pattern of leaves on its face.

I come from the lace of broken moonlight.
Where else would I belong?

Starlight on Waves

A sound of blackbirds in eucalyptus,
of redwings or violin strings.
The storm idles over the mountain
revealing, dissolving the same way
bird song and string song. That is why starlight,
called from hiding in cobalt and feathers,
plays the waves like notes,
or the words of a child's book –
lessons concealed, lessons divulged –
one word emerging from its fellows
to unroll its syllables – suddenly everywhere.

❊ ❊ ❊

Listening to a Mendelssohn piano trio,
I am carried to a bridge that leads
to a world of unbreakable light.
I want to stay on the bridge and listen
to the way cello and violin touch and separate.
How the narrating piano behind them
sometimes interrupts, sometimes protects.
A repetition of melody, the same and different –
urgent like the notes of starlight on waves,
green as the sliver of lime in a glass.
Ice light and lamp light.

❊ ❊ ❊

My hungry heart always wants to stay,
wants another twelve years with you
to add to our fifty, even though the sea
has played all its notes of blue and lavender.
I want one more book to read, one more day to write
the way a child writes, above the lines,
as if all words weren't written on water;
I want to live on the bridge that music makes,
listening to some enormity, elsewhere but not far.
Bridge that crosses and scatters the dark.

Stone and Desire

At dusk when stone could crack open,
here comes that final fluted song –
all spiral and treble.
The leaf banked cardinal has unlocked
the sudden slim tunnel of its throat.

All evening the luna moths
cross thresholds of lily and hibiscus.
Bees nudge deep beyond orange clutches
of petals into widening honeysuckle emptiness.
Such forays like our own into the body,
deep notes of need.

We enter the liquid longing
of the cardinal's twilight song.

In a Time of Distancing
For Tim

Sometimes I just want to touch you
when I'm caught in the honeyed notes of the cello,
or hearing the chorus of gulls quarrel
at low-tide feast, the drumming of surf
in their throats.

I live in the silence between notes,
between whistle-cries of the finches,
in the caesura of being present.

The world wants to be loved.
Andrea Bocelli sings for us
in hollow glitter of Milan Cathedral.

On the steps in front of soaring doors
and statues of the saved, he sings,
I was blind but now I see,

while cities without people flash on screen –
the Seine with no bookstalls,
Trafalgar with no traffic,
Times Square, a crazy tunnel echoing
the in-your-face circus that was.

The space, between Tibetan bowl moon
and lavender sea, buzzes with ions.
In the opera of what we're living through,
you help me stay grounded when stars call.
I touch you in the spaces of my longing.

Blue Distance

Let's walk along Clamshell shore
the way we did so many summers.
Let's sit on the dock, feet in water
watching white birches tremble
in the glassy lake.

Here, my younger self calls to my life now.
Here is the young wife and mother I was.
Listen – the voices of children
who once were our own.

In the still waters of the bay,
reflections of birches
soften as lamplight is softened
in water's live shiver.

This is the place where our marriage
ended and began again.
Remember how lost we were.
Now anger spins itself out
in the gyre of past.

No time for future to repeat
the way every acorn and leaf
of the oak trees repeat.

Look, how the great blue heron,
on a dead oak limb,
stares into the weed-dark
mirror of the lake.

What we see when we gaze
long enough into the blue –
years flowing through us, my love,
making more of us than we can know.

Our Story

I was from down the hill, West Seventh's
huddled houses under Highland Park's
frowning doors and windows.

You were up the hill, that neighborhood
of churches like forts, tree-lined playgrounds.

Around Highland pool you charged, pushing us
girls screaming into the deep end. Your blond hair
bleached by sun. My pale skin reddening like my
Irish grandmas, black hair dripping.

Somehow I knew even then
that fate would circle us round,
when we were grown.

❋ ❋ ❋

Later, newly sprung from the convent, I had just
stumbled out of that bleak house
in Nordeast, free in butterfly yellow, no more
under the unblinking stare of my Superior.

One night in Dinkytown I asked a friend if he knew
a man with a beautiful soul and he called you,
fresh out of the Christian Brothers.

Remember how we drove together
to the Brothers' house on Summit to pick up
the papers releasing you from vows?
Your Superior predicted you'd end up
washing dishes somewhere.

We were a run-on sentence, escaping religion,
a winter that would not end, a road
with a single direction.

With a comma moon above us,
we merged like two worlds, two words.

Fifty years later, it's just you and me
through long, sun baked summers
and years washing dishes together,
slowing the night's long phrases
with our full stop bodies.

A Medieval Herbal

I

Let the girl drink out of a church bell
yarrow lupine lichen   betony.
Let her sing while she drinks:
Beati Immaculati.

Let her remain a virgin
until twenty-seven or eight
until she finds her true origin.
Let her drink fennel against folly.

For heartache, give brambles –
pound the leaves, lay them over the breast
of both male and female.

II

In her thirties when she is thirsty,
she should climb the Tor of St. Catherine,
pick purple monkshood, beware the poison
in the root, but taste true passion.

At forty she will explode with pleasure.
Give her the spirit; plant parsley in good measure.
Periwinkle brings her grace; campion, victory.

Give her marigold in the church
after she betrays her matrimony.
That herb of decision-making
will not let her go until desire is spent.

III

At fifty her body quiets,
but she is not ready to stop.
Rosemary cures impotence
for men and women both.

Blessed be carnations
for they are the flowers of god.
Grow pansies, love's casualty.

IV

At sixty she finds wild roses,
signs of endurance and long life.
Bluebells beneath beech trees
remind her of his eyes.

At seventy spider webs brush
against her face after rain.
She touches the fuzziness
of late summer leaves.
Her own skin finely furred,
the hairs catch water.

At eighty, she lives without rue,
low growing, bell shaped,
rain and sun touch all of her.

Blueing

The blue eye charms in every Turkish market,
to ward off evil, the same periwinkle on doors
in every hill village in Portugal.
Blue squeezed from leaves
of the yellow flowering woad plant.

The same woad blue the Picts used
to paint their bodies
like the blue nude by Matisse
and the bodies of Cezanne's bathers –
blue blotched the way the sky
is cloud blotched.

❈ ❈ ❈

Lapis lazuli, original blue mined from earth
in Afghanistan, ground to aquamarine of illuminations,
found in the teeth of a medieval female
scribe, ground to paint the Virgin's gown
in centuries of Annunciations.

Fra Angelico's blue of Mary's gown, sky flowing.
The angel all tenderness – longing rains
over his ambiguous face. Her whole body
a question – all tilt, eyes frightened,
forgotten book dropped in the lap.

Once, a blue fog rose on the lake
revealing a fishing boat. I heard the whine
of its motor before I saw my children
wave their small arms –
turning wings loved by azure wind
bringing them home to me.

❊ ❊ ❊

Earth gave us blue.
Cobalt above and within all things.

In my mind, the hands and arms
that hold me wear the pregnant
blue of the sea before sunset.
For a moment, sky and earth
the same aquamarine.

We are blue smoke, mineral, ether
temporary against eternal hills.
Blue-veined sky breathes birds
in and out of the light,
their breasts glowing sapphires.

❊ ❊ ❊

At closing time, when the guard comes
into the empty Prado, I'm still leaning
into that impossible blue of the Virgin,
into that deepening sky.

From Water

The human spirit is made from water...
— Jorge Luis Borges

This morning I do nothing
but breathe and listen to the sea,
sink into a diamond path,
a net of light that swallows islands
below lion moon fading in the west.

This morning I want to be that place
where outer and inner meet –
the sea inside me, the same
sea that washes my senses
with sun blast and wave crash,
plovers surrounding pelican,
heron unrattled by gulls.

The palm tree's roots
that waves lave so often
the trunk stretches
its spirit, like mine,
leaning out over water.

Sun casts a glittering constellation,
past, present, what's to come —
all of it seamless, sudden blooming
from rock and sand,
a tide pool erupting with anemones.

Shudder of heron-shadow
over bottomless flow that holds
estuary, bridge, gate,
tonight's Orion and Cassiopeia,

red frog in Costa Rica,
blue dragonfly, palm tree on the edge –

awash in the wild, patient light –
our beginning and our end.

Publication Acknowledgements

NEW POEMS

Thank you to David Horvitz, whose art book, *change the name of the days*, inspired several new poems.

Thank you to the editors of these zines, anthologies and community arts organizations for selecting these poems, sometimes in different versions, for publication:

American Writers Literary Review, Witches' Solstice ;
Anacapa Review, also in *Rewilding Hope – Cracked Walnut Anthology*,
    Welcoming Night;
California Quarterly, Go in Deep;
Gyroscope Review, Eighty, Adamantine;
League of MN Poets, Look Now, posted on Richfield Lake walking path ;
    (contest winner)
MN Center for Book Arts, Pelicans in the Rain,
Monterey Poetry Review, Listen to the Sea, See Through the Eyes of a
    Crow, Hope in All Things;
Poetry Breakfast, Ocean's Edge;
Poured Out from the Big Dipper – Blue Light Press, Against the Night: A Poem Sequence;
St. Paul Almanac online, Diagrammer of Sentences
(a winner of the Breakthrough contest);
Salt, Son et Lumiére: Chartre, My Cartographic History;
Solo Voyage, Bridges, Done;
Wising Up Press Anthologies – Pause, Winter Solstice in Big Sur; *Adult Children*, Son et Lumiére: Chartre ; *Wholeness*, Welcoming Night.

I wish to thank the editors of the following publications in which the poems selected from *This Body She's Entered, The Long Journey into North, Green Journey/Red Bird, Illuminations, Love in the End, What's Left is the Singing, The Lifeline Trembles, Cypher Garden and Nocturnes: Between Flesh and Stone* first appeared, a few in slightly different versions. Thank you for your encouragement. Thank you to David Horvitz, whose art book, change the name of the days, inspired several new poems.

JOURNALS

Alaska Quarterly Review;
ArtLife: (Collaborations with painter, Hervé Constant);
Askew; Bloomsbury Review; BoomerLitMag;
Dust and Fire; Ekphrasis; Ekphrastic Review; Great River Review;
Gyroscope Review; Journal of Language and Literacy Education; Lake Street Review;
Loonfeather; Luna; Nimrod: Boatyard, Late October, In the Margins – A poem sequence, Histories, Parakeet, The Heart in its Cage of Bone, Illuminator Dreams, Lost, A Sisters Story, Cypher Garden (all semi-finalists and finalists for the Pablo Neruda Award); *Miramar; Northeast; Packinghouse Review; Persimmon Tree:* Names for Green (2010 contest winner); *Pirene's Fountain; Rock & Sling; St. Paul Almanac; Salt; Sidewalks; Spillway; Visions International; Water-Stone Review; Whistling Shade.*

ANTHOLOGIES

And the Humming: Poems About Grandparents;
Between Stone and Flesh: Anthology of Winners of 2002 Lake Superior Writers Prize;
Broad Wings, Long Legs: A Rookery of Heron Poems (James Silas Rogers, ed);
Carrying the Branch: Poets in Search of Peace (Glass Lyre Press);
First Water: Best of Pirene's Fountain;
Meditations on Divine Names (Moonrise Press);
Midwestern Women Poets;
New Poetry from the Midwest;
Rocked by the Waters: Poems of Motherhood (Nodin Press);
Saturday's Women Anthology; The Silk Road (Pirene's Fountain;
The Wind Blows, the Ice Breaks: Poems of Loss and Renewal;
Thirty-Three Minnesota Poets (Nodin Press, 2000);
To Sing Along the Way: Minnesota Women Poets from Pre-Territorial Days to the Present;
We Are Here: Village Poets Anthology;
Wising Up Press Anthologies: Creativity & Constraint, Daring to Repair, Crossing Class;
Woman in Metaphor: an anthology of poems inspired by the paintings Of Stephen Linsteadt: Wounded Angel;
What Light (Bright Hill Press Anniversary Anthology).

Birches appeared in *The Long Journey Into North:* A limited edition chapbook By Juniper Press.

In the Middle was reprinted in *Becoming a Teacher in the New Society* edited by Mary Kay Rummel and Elizabeth Quintero and published by Peter Lang International.

Cairns was part of a dance performance choreographed by Lisa McKhann in Duluth, MN as part of Lake Superiors Writers prize.

Hallowed Ground: In search of Ireland's unworldly sites, an arist's book by painter Gaal Shepherd included Field Walking in County Donegal and What Stone Knows.

Many of these poems have been performed with pianist, Gwen Perun.

SELECTED AWARDS

Loft Mentor Award;
Irish American Crossroads Prize: Ars Poetica, What Stone Knows;
Minnesota Voices Award from New Rivers Press;
Finalist for Minnesota Book Award
Ventura Country Writers Prize; Ten Pushcart Prize nominations including for A Beltane Tapestry, The Poet Goes Fishing,
Cypher Garden, Still Life with Lemons, As if, Palimpsest;
Lake Superior Writers Prize; Laureate's Choice, Maria Faust sonnet competition;
Diane Glancy Poetry Award from Dust and Fire;
Residency Awards: Norcroft, Anderson Center, Vermont Studio Center, St. John's University; American Academy of Arts and Letters in Rome.

About the Author

Mary Kay Rummel, grew up in St. Paul near the Mississippi and the corner where Montreal, Lexington and West Seventh meet near Highland Park. She was the first Poet Laureate of Ventura County, CA. *Little River of Amazements: New and Selected Poems* is her tenth published poetry book, her eighth full collection. Blue Light Press also published *Nocturnes: Between Flesh and Stone*, *Cypher Garden*, *The Lifeline Trembles*, as a winner of the 2014 Blue Light Press Award and *What's Left is the Singing*. *This Body She's Entered*, her first book, won the Minnesota Voices Award for poetry and was published by New Rivers Press in 1989. It was a finalist for the Minnesota Book Award. She was a recipient of a Loft Mentor award. Her work has appeared in numerous regional, national and international literary journals and anthologies and has received several awards, including ten Pushcart nominations. She was a co-editor of *Psalms of Cinder & Silt*, a collection of community poems related to recent California wildfires published by Glenna Luschei at Solo Press. Her poems have been published in many journals and anthologies centered in both California and the Midwest including *Water~Stone Review*, *Alaska Quarterly Review*, *MiraMar*, *Anacapa Review*, *Gyroscope Review*, *Conestoga Zen*, *Pirene's Fountain*, *Salt*, *Askew*, *Spillway* and as a frequent finalist for the Pablo Neruda Prize, in *Nimrod*.

Mary Kay has read her poems in many venues in the US, England and Ireland and has been a featured reader at poetry festivals including in the Ojai Poetry Festival and San Luis Obisbo Poetry Fest. She has participated in numerous poetry residencies including Anderson House and Vermont Studio Center and performs poetry with musicians. She has collaborated with artists in the US and England, most recently at the Minnesota Center for Book Arts. A Professor Emerita from the University of Minnesota, Duluth, Mary Kay also taught at the University of Minnesota, Minneapolis, and at California State University, Channel Islands.

She is a founding board member of the nonprofit Ventura County Poetry Project. She and her husband, Conrad (Tim), live in California and Minnesota, near children and grandchildren in both states. She can be contacted through email at marykayrummel.com.

Books by Mary Kay Rummel

POETRY

This Body She's Entered. New Rivers Press (1989).
winner of Minnesota Voices Award
Finalist, Minnesota Book Award
Editor: Bill Truesdale, Vivian Balfour

Long Journey Into North: a chapbook. Juniper Press (1998)
Editor, John Judson

Green Journey, Red Bird. Loonfeather Press (2000)
Editor, Betty Rossi

The Illuminations. Cherry Grove Collections (2006)
Editors, Kevin Walzer, Lori Jareo

Love in the End: a chapbook. Bright Hill Press (2008)
Editor: Bertha Rogers

What's Left is the Singing. Blue Light Press (2014)
Editor, Diane Frank

The Lifeline Trembles. Blue Light Press (2017)
Winner of the 2014 Blue Light Book Award
Editor: Diane Frank

Cypher Garden. Blue Light Press (2017)
Editor: Diane Frank

Nocturnes: Between Flesh and Stone. Blue Light Press (2020)
Editor: Diane Frank

NONFICTION

Written with Elizabeth Quintero

Teachers' Reading, Teachers' Lives. Suny Press (1996)

American Voices: Webs of Diversity. Prentice Hall Inc. (1998)

Becoming a Teacher in the New Society. Peter Lang Publishing Inc. New York (2003)

Storying: A Path to Our Future. Peter Lang Publishing Inc: New York (2015)

www.ingramcontent.com/pod-product-compliance
Lightning Source LLC
Chambersburg PA
CBHW022006160426
43197CB00007B/295